SHIPPING CONTAINER HOME

ANTONY BON

INTRODUCTION

Container homes are simply what they sound like: homes constructed from steel shipping containers that you see on trucks, trains, and ships transporting goods worldwide. People are constructing homes of all shapes and sizes out of these massive Lego blocks.

Shipping containers are generally available in 10ft, 20ft, and 40ft. The smallest shipping container may provide around 100 square feet of floor space for a shipping container home. Eight larger containers can be combined to form a two-story house with a floor area of around 1400 square feet. Hundreds of container micro-apartments can be combined to form a large apartment building.

What are the advantages of using shipping containers to build apartments, studios, offices, and cabins? There are about 14 million 'out-of-service' containers in the country, so there is plenty to go around. And there's something about giant blocks that appeals to me!

Aside from being trendy, interest in container homes is part of a broader movement toward prefabricated and modular homes as a way to save money. A lot of potential homeowners want to save money on building and maintenance. There's also a perception that container homes help with recycling.

What is a shipping container house?

A shipping container house is any structure built out of a shipping container, but the resulting structures can be varied. Shipping containers are usually 20 feet by 8 feet or 40 feet by 8 feet in size. The smaller container provides approximately 160 square feet of living space, while the larger container provides 320 square feet. There are two height choices: standard (8.5 feet high) or high cube (approximately a foot of additional vertical living space). Some shipping container homes stop here, converting the small spaces into tiny homes or offices.

However, many builders and homeowners, including this one in Missouri, combine containers to make larger houses. Walls are often demolished to build more spacious interiors in homes with many containers, and conventional building techniques add exterior materials and additional rooms.

Some containers can be stacked to create multi-level homes, while others can be twisted and turned Jenga-style to create stunning architectural masterpieces.

The Advantages of Shipping Container Homes

1.   Prefab Shipping Container Homes

Many shipping container homes are available as prefabricated modular homes, making construction time shorter. Some organizations advertise delivery in as little as ten weeks! The majority of building code inspections are completed at the factory, which simplifies and expedites the process. If you're building a do-it-yourself project or designing a custom home, the container provides a pleasant pre-built framework to work with.

2.   Ease of Transport and Finding a Site

Moving containers around the world are possible thanks to a global infrastructure. Once they arrive at your place, they are reasonably easy to install on a prepared foundation.

3.   Shipping Container Homes Have Predictable Costs

The majority of the job is completed on a factory floor for a fixed price. The only variable costs are delivery to the site, foundation, site preparation, assembly, and utility connections. Container houses, on the other hand, are not necessarily less costly. Estimates differ, and some say you'll save 5-10%, depending on what you're comparing to.

4. Recycled Shipping Container Homes

The environmental appeal of a container home stems from the fact that you are repurposing a shipping industry byproduct to create a home. This can be beneficial, but as we can see, it is not always the case or the best option.

Some of the benefits, such as speed of construction and predictable pricing, apply to all prefabricated and modular houses, not just those built with shipping containers. Container homes, on the other hand, benefit from the global infrastructure designed to transport shipping containers. Also, critics agree that container homes can be useful when local building expertise is lacking, or emergency shelters need to be transported quickly. The flexibility of container transportation is a major benefit in these scenarios.

Container homes are often advertised as environmentally friendly because they are claimed to be constructed from recycled containers, conserving metal resources. There are many old shipping containers out there that are no longer in use, and converting them into homes has many appeals. But, in terms of sustainability, is a container home the best use of a container? Many people would disagree.

Disadvantages of Shipping Container Homes

1. Shipping Container Homes Are Not Always Effective Recycling

Most factory-built container homes are made from 'one-use containers that have only been used once. These containers are usually in good condition, with no dents or rust, and are thus better for building with than containers that have been deemed "out-of-service" and may have been damaged over time. Taking a box with a long shipping life out of service after a single use is not effective recycling. And a container contains much more steel than is needed to construct a house; if recycled as steel, it could provide enough steel studs for 14 framed houses of the same size.

2. Shipping Container Homes Could Have Structural Issues

The corners of a shipping container are very strong, but the roof isn't, so you'll usually need to build another roof over it, particularly if there will be snow. The corrugated steel walls are also crucial to the structure's resilience. This means that new reinforcement is needed every time a wide window or door opening is cut out. When they're stacked to make bigger houses, welded (expensive) reinforcement is needed anywhere two containers meet in a non-corner spot. Any future renovations will require extensive engineering and welding.

3. Are Shipping Container Homes Safe?

It's always impossible to tell what was shipped in a used container – anything from common household items to dangerous industrial products – or what it's been through. Since the paints and finishes used on containers are industrial and designed for shipping across the ocean rather than for residential use, they can contain lead and toxic pesticides.

What Is The Standard Size of a Shipping Container Home?

The size of shipping containers is limited, and plumbing, HVAC, insulation, and other systems will quickly consume them. Since a container was made to fit on a train, it's narrow, and regular furniture won't fit. A typical container is also just 8 feet wide and 8 feet 6 inches tall, leaving little headroom after insulation and wiring.

How Do You Insulate a Shipping Container Home?

The shape of a shipping container makes it difficult to insulate the exterior properly. A relatively thin layer of insulation with a high R-value per inch, such as polyurethane spray foam, is mostly used to avoid taking up interior space. While spray foam is an efficient and airtight insulator, the blowing agents used in many brands of spray foam are powerful greenhouse gases.

Costs Of Shipping Containers Homes

So, what will a shipping container home cost? Container homes that are smaller and more basic will cost between $10,000 to $35,000. Large homes with multiple shipping containers and amenities will cost between $100,000 and $175,000 to build. In certain cases, shipping container homes are half the price per square foot of conventional stick-built homes. However, comparing apples to apples is difficult, as there are several variables to consider.

So, what can increase the cost? Although land costs and climate requirements are important factors, other factors to consider include:

• Size, design, layout, and the number of containers required

• Cleaning cost if the container is used

• Welding and Fabrication requirements

• Plumbing and electrical

• Kitchen and bathroom finishes

• Lofts

* Siding

* Flooring

* Windows

* Insulation

* Doors

* and more.

An engineer in Canada builds a basic shipping container home for only $20,000. On the other hand, a pre-fabricated container house has a price tag comparable to a normal home.

How Long Does A Shipping Container Home Last?

Shipping container homes should last at least 25 years, but they can last much longer if they are well-maintained or have siding on the outside. The most common problem that can shorten the life of a shipping container home is rust. It's important to check and search for rust spots in your shipping container house. To prevent rust from spreading, any problem areas should be treated and fixed.

Why shipping containers homes?

Like other new products, the shipping container was designed to solve a problem: moving goods efficiently and safely through land and sea. Of course, humans had been doing so for thousands of years, but in inefficient ways most of the time.

The crucial innovation of containers was that they were:

- Large enough to carry thousands of cubic feet of merchandise while still being small enough to fit on a truck and travel on regular roads.
- Uniform enough that any truck or ship could carry any container, but versatile enough that they could be used for dry goods, refrigerated goods, bulk liquids, and so on.
- Strong enough to withstand an often perilous voyage at sea but light enough to be moved with cranes, forklifts, and other material handling equipment

The planet has been changed by the economic transport of goods from distant countries, thanks to the work of people like Malcolm McLean, in just a few short decades. Steel shipping containers were a key component in making it possible.

Consider how convenient it would be to fly anywhere globally and use the same type of plug or make transactions in the same currency. It isn't easy to achieve this degree of global standardization, but that's exactly what shipping containers have done!

McLean could not have anticipated the gradual accumulation of surplus containers as a result of trade imbalances. In the 1980s, this and other factors prompted pioneers to investigate converting shipping containers into usable structures. We now have thousands of examples of amazing container structures thanks to the imagination of both talented designers and ordinary people like you.

Are container homes legal in all countries?

Shipping container homes can be found in various countries worldwide, including the United Kingdom, the United States,

China, Indonesia, Vietnam, Tasmania, and Denmark. In most countries, shipping container homes are allowed. However, there are some restrictions. If you want to live in a container as a permanent residence in the UK, for example, you'll need to apply for planning permission. If your container home is in an area of outstanding beauty, you may also need planning permission. Container homes must also adhere to all relevant local building regulations. Because the laws governing container homes differ from country to country, it is usually a good idea to seek advice from your local government before embarking on a container conversion project.

CHAPTER 1: HISTORY OF SHIPPING CONTAINER HOMES

People take shipping containers for granted. Yes, you see them stacked up at ports from time to time, but it's easy to forget that practically every consumer goods you use were presumably transported in a shipping container.

You have to go back a few decades to identify a time when shipping containers and intermodal transportation networks did not exist. Innovators in the recent past have recognized the potential of shipping containers to construct homes and other structures.

Even if you aren't a history buff, there is interesting information on how economic needs influenced the size, shape, and proliferation of containers available today.

We'll look at how shipping was done before containers were invented, how and who invented them, the impact they've had on globalization, and how they've swiftly increased in favor of building materials.

The World Before Shipping Containers

For millennia, humanity has sailed the oceans, bringing with them not only people but also food, cotton, treasure, and goods that their own country had never seen before. Think of the Egyptians, the Romans, the Greeks, and, most recently, the British!

What method did they use to convey their wares around the globe? They shipped to other nations, but the process was long and difficult due to a lack of uniformity.

Goods would be held at a port warehouse until a boat was available. These goods would be carried from the warehouse to the side of the docked ship when an empty vessel arrived. Typically, goods would be piled into sacks, bales, boxes, and barrels and then manually loaded onto the ship. As you can expect, this was a time-consuming operation. Breakbulk freight was the term for this process. Around 200,000 pieces of goods would be onboard an average ship.

This lack of uniformity became a serious problem at the end of the second industrial revolution (the early 1900s), especially given how common trains had now become. Transferring cargo from ships to trains was extraordinarily slow, causing massive delays and blockades in several ports. Unloading and reloading larger ships would take around a week.

This was the only way to move things, and the technique stayed unaltered for generations.

The Incredible Vision of Malcolm McLean

There was a pressing need for a standardized mode of transportation, but this necessitated the alignment of several industries, including ships, railroads, trucks, and port terminals. As you can imagine, such a feat would require a great deal of effort and persuasion.

While Henry Ford is well-known around the world, Malcolm McLean is virtually unknown. You'll understand why he was such an essential contributor to the world in just a few minutes.

Malcolm McLean was born in 1914 and grew up on a farm in North Carolina. After graduating from high school in 1931, he worked for several years to save enough money to buy a used truck. He started his transportation company in 1934. McLean quickly expanded his transportation company, and by the end of the year, he had five trucks working for him.

During a regular transfer of cotton bales from North Carolina to New Jersey in 1937, McLean watched dockworkers loading and unloading cargo, which took hours upon hours. He reflected on how much of a waste of time and money this was.

McLean focused on his transportation company, which had over 1,750 trucks and 37 transport terminals, from 1937 to 1950. It was, in fact, the fifth-largest truck transportation company in the United States.

Several weight limitations and levying fines were implemented on-road vehicles during this period. McLean's drivers were often fined for transporting hefty loads of cargo.

McLean was looking for a more effective way to carry his clients' cargo when he remembered what happened in New Jersey in 1937. This was when he came up with the idea of designing a standard-sized trailer that could be loaded onto boats in hundreds rather than just one or two, as he did with his vehicles. He envisioned eliminating most of his vehicles and replacing them with boats to convey goods to strategically placed trucking hubs, thus modernizing his transportation industry.

This would mean that trucks would only be used for short intrastate deliveries, removing the weight limitations and fees implemented recently.

Intermodal Transport Shifts From Idea To Reality

McLean sold his trucking company after being persuaded by his idea to develop a standardized shipping trailer or container. He took out a $42 million bank loan in 1955. He used $7 million of the loan to buy Pan-Atlantic Steamship Company, an established shipping company. Many of the eastern port cities that McLean was pursuing already had Pan-Atlantic docking rights. He renamed the company SeaLand Industries shortly after purchasing them.

McLean collaborated with engineer Keith Tantlinger to design, improve, and test many container designs before settling on a primitive version of what we now know as a shipping container. It was theft-resistant because it was sturdy, stackable, standardized, easy to load and unload, and lockable.

Now that McLean had his containers, the final piece of the jigsaw puzzle was to create ships to transport them. He purchased the oil tanker Ideal X and modified it to carry 58 of his newly built containers and 15,000 tons of petroleum.

Ideal X departed New Jersey on April 26, 1956, headed for Houston. The company was taking orders before the ship even docked in Houston to transport items back to New Jersey, proving the success of his plan. This was largely due to McLean's ability to provide a 25% savings on the cost of traditional cargo transportation at the time. Furthermore, because the containers were lockable, goods could not be stolen while in transit.

Following the Ideal X's first trip, McLean ordered the Gateway City, the world's first container ship.

The inaugural journey of the Gateway City was from New Jersey to Miami in October 1957. Unbelievably, just two sets of dockworkers were needed to unload and load the cargo. The cargo could be moved at an incredible 30 tons per hour, which was unprecedented at the time.

Standardization of Containers

McLean was using 35-foot containers at the time rather than the 20 and 40-foot containers we see now.

The lack of consistency in terms of container size and corner fittings, however, remained an issue. This homogeneity was required to stack containers efficiently. Furthermore, railroads, trucks, and other modes of transportation required a standard-sized container so that each mode of transportation could be designed to a single size.

During the Vietnam War, the United States government sought a more effective way to ship goods and pushed for standardization. McLean's SeaLand Industries was still using 35-foot containers, while Matson's, a competitor in the business, was using 24-foot containers. McLean agreed to release his patent of the revolutionary shipping container corner posts (essential to its stacking and strength), and several standards were agreed upon:

• January 1968: ISO 668 defined the dimensions, terminology, and ratings.

• July 1968: ISO 790 was established to clarify how containers should be identified (Replaced by ISO 6346).

We currently have the 20-foot and 40-foot shipping containers and a few other less frequent sizes due to these standards. The Twenty-foot Equivalent Unit (TEU), or 20-foot container, became the industry standard for referencing cargo volume.

Why did building with shipping containers become a trend?

In a moment, we'll look at some of the earliest people to think about using containers for construction. First, let's talk about why that idea was even worth discussing in the first place.

In many Western countries, including the United States, we import far more than we export. We don't use the shipping container to bring things into the country, and we don't use it to ship goods out. This implies that there is a surplus of shipping containers.

How much of a surplus?

According to the US Department of Transportation's Maritime Administration, the US imported 17,541,120 TEUs in 2012. However, only 11,935,906 TEUs were exported (Source).

TEU stands for a twenty-foot equivalent unit and is a measuring unit. A TEU is the same size as a conventional 20-foot shipping container.

There was a surplus of more than 5 million 20-foot shipping containers. Not every shipping container is still in the United States. It would be worthwhile to return new containers to Asia for reuse, yet there are still many containers in the United States.

This trend has been going on for a long time, and we've taken a look at some recent data from the Maritime Administration of the US Department of Transportation:

Year	2008	2009	2010	2011	2012
Total Export (TEUs)	11,332,821	10,362,483	11,240,344	11,952,135	11,935,906
Total Import (TEUs)	17,120,767	14,541,415	16,626,033	17,077,443	17,541,120
Net Difference	5,787,946	4,178,932	5,385,690	5,125,308	5,605,214

Since we have such a large surplus, couldn't we just recycle the shipping containers we have in the US?

The answer is that melting them down and turning them into other steel products is usually inefficient.

Alternative Uses for Shipping Containers

If we search for the first official record of a shipping container home, we find a man named Phillip Clark. Clark filed a patent on the "Method for transforming one or more steel shipping containers into a habitable building" on November 23, 1987.

He asserted that the ideal modular building material. He also mentioned that reused shipping containers could be utilized to build affordable residences.

The patent took two years to be granted. Clark received his

authorized patent #US4854094A on Tuesday, August 8, 1989.

So, how did Phillip Clark come up with his concept? Was he the first to suggest that shipping containers may be used to construct houses?

Not at all. Shipping containers found their way onto the big screen just two years before Clark's patent was submitted. Shipping containers were utilized to construct various buildings on the set of the 1985 film Space Rage.

We may go even further back to the 1970s, when Nicholas Lacey, a British architect, wrote his university thesis on the subject of reusing shipping containers and converting them into livable spaces.

Since then, he's worked with Urban Space Management to develop a number of these shipping container structures.

Starting in 1962, we may still see examples of shipping containers being reused as buildings.

Insbrandtsen Company Inc. submitted a patent titled "Combination shipping container and showcase" on Friday, October 12, 1962. Within this patent, Christopher Betjemann was listed as the inventor, and it argues that shipping containers can be utilized as an exhibition booth when companies tour and showcase their products.

Patent #US3182424A was granted on Tuesday, May 11, 1965.

Going Mainstream

Stewart Brand, an American writer, released the book "How Buildings Learn" in 1994. A brand goes on to write ideas for converting shipping containers into office space in the book. This was the first book to mention shipping container building.

From here, shipping container homes started gaining momentum, with the "The Simon's Town High School Hostel" being the first finished project we could find on record.

Safmarine donated forty reused shipping containers to Simon's Town High School, which sparked the project. The school intended to use the containers to construct a hostel that could accommodate 120 students at any given time. The project cost $227,000 in total and was opened to the public on November 30, 1998.

21st Century Shipping Container Homes

In 2006, the first shipping container home in the United States was designed by Peter DeMaria, a Californian architect.

The Redondo Beach House was built in 2007 and was approved under the national Uniform Building Code (one of the predecessors of the IBC). This was the world's first real shipping container home.

We've seen shipping container homes spring up all over the world since then! Some of the most well-known ones are:

Container Guest House (2010)

Texas-based Poteet Architects designed this home. It's made out of a 40-foot shipping container reused to provide 320 square feet of living space.

Containers of Hope (2011)

Containers of Hope was built in Costa Rica for roughly $40,000 and is known for its tremendous cost reductions. The home, which was constructed using numerous shipping containers, is passively cooled with a sloped roof.

The Caterpillar House (2012)

Sebastián Irarrázaval designed and built this home in Chile. The home has a land area of 3,800 square feet and was built from 12 containers. It was constructed on a mountainside just outside of Santiago, providing the owners with breathtaking views!

The popularity of shipping container homes continues to grow, and there appears to be no end in sight for these environmentally friendly, low-cost homes.

As the popularity of shipping container homes increases, we've seen various other creative uses for shipping containers, including restaurants, offices, and schools.

Chapter 2: LAWS AND PERMITS

If you're interested in shipping container homes, it's a good idea to investigate the local container home laws and regulations in your area.

This is the safest way to ensure that you would not breach any regulations if you start building a home out of shipping containers. The guidelines presented below are intended to provide you with valuable information and shed light on this situation.

Although shipping containers were designed with a specific function in mind, many people found their incredible potential for repurposing to transport large quantities of products worldwide.

It's easy to see why some people considered using them for home construction because they were engineered to be sturdy and durable, with a capacity of up to 55,000 lbs.

The demand for shipping container houses grew due to the concept of recycling and repurposing large metal containers, having a new and unique looking home, and the flexibility promised by this solution. In today's world, the construction industry alone is worth many billions of dollars.

However, without the necessary permits, shipping containers cannot be used to build a house. Permits cannot be obtained until the containers have been licensed by the regulatory bodies in charge of this region.

Who are the regulatory bodies that have the authority to grant the required approvals? The conversion of shipping containers into units suitable for human habitation is governed by the International Residential Code and the International Building Code. The International Code Council was the first organization to provide an official guideline for using shipping containers in commercial and residential construction.

This guideline was issued in February 2016, and it is called ICC-ES AC462. The Modular Building Institute and the National Portable Storage Association are likely to influence future regulations. Even then, most of the regulations in this field are provided by local building code bodies, so it's worth checking them out.

What Kind of Permits Do I Need for Shipping Container House?

Everything starts with a design, just like every other construction project. Ideally, you can enlist the assistance of a skilled designer who can create the perfect design for your shipping container home while considering the environment in which you reside. Still, it's best not to proceed to anything complex or spend too much money before speaking with a local municipality representative.

Since local regulations can vary from those issued by the state, it's best to figure this out before you start spending consistent amounts of money on your dream. Presenting a professional design to the building commissioner, on the other hand, would show that you are determined and committed to uphold the requirements and construct a reliable home from the onset.

You will be asked to show a paper containing the technical requirements and a technical drawing of the containers you are about to use. This is typically required so that authorities can determine if the containers are appropriate for use as a residential structure. If this is a necessity, obtaining all of this information can be difficult because you would need to find the container manufacturer, which is, in most cases, located in China.

Since shipping containers are typically leased to various companies throughout their lives, you'll have to work your way down the line before you reach the container's provider. If you're fortunate, the supplier or manufacturer will be able to provide you with a specification sheet as well as a professional drawing.

Finally, you'll need permission from your local authorities. Even though shipping container homes are not a new concept, many areas are still unfamiliar with such requests and may not know how to handle your permit application. While finding the person issuing the permit can be difficult, it is always a good idea to start by speaking with the person in charge of building permits in your area. A building permit isn't always required, so if that's the case for you, skip this section and get to work on your shipping container house.

Container Home Laws – Is it Legal to Build Shipping Container Home in My state?

A shipping container home could be one of the most cost-effective ways for many Americans to have the home of their dreams finally. But, before you put this on your wish list, make sure it's legal to build a home like this in your state. As a result, the issue of whether or not building a shipping container home is legal in your state arises.

The answer to this question is that most states in the U.S allow the building of homes out of shipping containers. Many of those who don't allow it yet consider it and look for ways to regulate it properly.

Bear in mind that even if your state permits the building of shipping container homes, your city may not. So, once again, check your local laws on this issue. To learn about the legal terms in your state, you'll need to contact the county or city planner to check their recommendations in this situation.

Even if you get permission from the planner to construct a shipping container house, you must also adhere to local zoning and building codes.

What are Shipping Container Building Codes?

Aside from zoning, you'll need to be aware of building codes. This is critical because a code would tell you what criteria should be followed when constructing something in a specific region. As a result, you won't construct a structure that does not comply with the building code in the region where you intend to build it.

One of the things you must prove when applying for a building permit is to follow the building code in the area where you intend to build your shipping container house. You will only get the approval you need if you can show that you will comply.

These building codes are generally issued by the International Residential Code and the International Building Code in the United States. They can also change once a year or twice a year, so it's worth double-checking these codes before you begin your construction project. Building codes are one of the first things you should review before coming up with a design for your shipping container home since certain states have their codes in this sector.

Can I Apply Online for Permits?

Yes, you can apply for a permit online if you know the department to submit your application and if you have all of the necessary documents. This is why speaking with someone from the municipality could be beneficial.

You'll learn more about the local laws governing shipping container homes, as well as what you'll need to get started building one. You can start collecting permits, finish your home's design, and everything else required to apply for a permit online once you have all of the details you need.

Obtaining a permit, regardless of its intent, is a time-consuming and patient process. Fortunately, you may obtain the permit you want online. By accessing online permits, you can apply for the permit you need conveniently and comfortably. However, double-check that you have everything you'll need to submit a qualified permit. This means you should already have all of the required approvals from your local legislation.

What is Shipping Container Zoning

Every state in the United States has its zoning regulations governing the areas available for building purposes. The zoning would specify the types of structures that can be constructed in a given location. The zones are designed to aid a city's development in a harmonious manner and accordance with the municipality's plans. Huston, for example, is an exception to this law since it does not have zoning. As a result, you should review the area's zoning code to build your shipping container home before getting started. The zoning code will tell you what types of structures are permitted in the region so that you can plan your future home accordingly.

CHAPTER 3: SITE PREPARATION

Before you send your containers to the building site, there is a surprising amount of site work to be done. If you don't think about and execute these things early in the project, you'll end up with many costly reworks later.

At a high level, the site planning and preparation you do now is meant to ensure that the land is ready for the building site, the building site is ready for the containers, and the containers are ready for your container home design and lifestyle. It's an essential part of the overall project planning for your container home building.

Many of the factors mentioned below interact with one another; changing one affects many others. In container home planning, finding the right balance between conflicting interests is a common theme, and this process is no exception.

Deciding on Location

Before you (or anyone else) begins actual work on your house, you must first determine where you want your container home to be mounted. There are a lot of things to think about, and some of them might already be on your mind subconsciously.

We think that having them written down allows you to be transparent and honest about the factors that influence your decision.

Sun and Shade

The sun may be both a blessing and a curse depending on your climate. It can warm you up on a chilly morning, but it can also cause you to become blind when drinking your morning coffee.

It can give your interior spaces a gentle, natural glow, but it can also induce solar thermal gain, necessitating more air conditioning.

Pay attention to how the sun interacts with and region on your property at various times of the day when you start to narrow down the possible building sites on your property.

Shade from nearby trees and bushes is important, but you can also be influenced by water reflections and how topography affects horizon elevation. Remember that the shade will be diminished when deciduous trees lose their leaves in the fall and winter.

You should also consider how the sun acts at various times of the year. In different seasons, the sun moves across the sky in a different trajectory depending on the latitude.

SunCalc is an excellent tool for calculating the sun's altitude over the horizon (in degrees) for every location on the globe at any time and date. It can also assist you in considering roof overhangs for doors and windows that protect from the hot summer sun while allowing in the warm winter sun.

Topography and Drainage

Topography and drainage, which are closely related, also need your attention. The form of the land is referred to as topography, and the way water flows through it is referred to as drainage. When assessing project locations, you must consider how it would be to live there and how it would be to build there.

Container homes usually do not need a slab foundation, which is one of their benefits. Because of their inherent strength, they can normally be supported only at their four corners and 'bridge over' any terrain changes if a level foundation system can be designed and installed underneath them. However, if access to building the foundation is restricted, this last step may be costly.

Topography has a strong influence on water and drainage. While having easy access to a pond or stream can sound appealing, consider the risk of flooding and how high the water may rise.

You may also have seasonal pools that form in low spots on the land and seasonal erosion that happens during heavy rains and threatens your foundation. Observing the property during a rainstorm will help you understand how water flows through it and what steps you may need to take to divert or contain it.

Water may also be a haven for insects such as mosquitos, harmful animals such as snakes, and noisy birds. So, once again, we suggest spending time exploring the land to learn how these factors can affect you.

Views

The view out, or what they see outside through the different windows and doors, is what most people think about when they think of their container home's view. A view of a valley, a distant mountain peak, a peaceful stream, or the city skyline can all add value to the livability of a container home. Making sure that you position and orient windows in a way that maximizes the views you can capture require some thought, but it's well worth it!

It's also interesting to think about the view from the inside, or what someone else (visitors, neighbors, or even your own family) would see if they looked inside. This is mostly about privacy and security concerns. You can have a problem if your neighbors can see into your bedroom or if your child's treehouse looks straight into your bathroom.

Another significant point to remember is the street view of your house. Changing the home's orientation about the street can greatly impact how it feels.

Some people prefer the house's long axis to be parallel to the street, whereas others prefer it to be perpendicular. If you have the room, you can place the house at an angle, enhancing the geometric design already provided by using containers.

Another option is to flip the design backward to change it up from what you originally planned.

You'll just have to see how much space you have for these options and how well they fit into your property and house design.

Setbacks and Restrictions

We spoke a lot about zoning and deed restrictions previously, and it's important to remember that these restrictions will impact where you build, even if it's on your land.

For example, the permissible height of your structure can be reduced as you get closer to a property line. Furthermore, you might be unable to build anything within a certain distance of a property line.

Before you commit to a construction site, make sure you consult with all relevant parties to ensure that what you're doing is legal. The longer you wait to find out, the costly it will be!

Access

The final part of the location requirements we'll discuss is site access. After all, a house is worthless if you can't get to it.

Unless you're going completely off the grid, we'll assume that your primary mode of transportation would be via automobile, which means you will need a road. The easiest road to construct is short, straight, and smooth, but this is impossible due to land constraints.

Consider how you'll get to your potential building site from the main road on the edge of your property. How much elevation change will there be, and how long will It be? Are there any steep slopes that must be smoothed, low points that must be crossed, or natural obstacles that must be navigated around?

What trees and other foliage would have to be cut down? Will the views improve or deteriorate as you travel up the lane, and will the changing seasons make the views better or worse?

Make sure you consider access not only for your vehicle but also for building trucks, large trailers hailing containers, and heavy machinery such as cranes. Will the road be broad enough for them to use, with gentle enough turns? Will it be flat enough for them to walk over without high-centering? Will the mud and water render them impassable for heavy vehicles?

After considering all of these factors, you may decide to change the route of your access road slightly before you find one that best suits your needs. Note that if you can't develop a single route that does it well, you can always build a second, temporary road for heavy machinery that will be demolished after the house is finished.

There are various options for site access, but you don't want to be bushwhacking new trails the day a contractor arrives because your road is inadequate.

Site work

All of the physical work you'll have to do to get your construction site and surrounding area ready falls under the category of site work. It may make sense to do one before the other, depending on the type of dirt moving needed, the utilities you need to install, and the direction of approach, so you don't break something with heavy equipment.

Marking and Staking

The first step is to mark the corners of the area where your shipping container home will be built, as well as the locations of all planned and current utilities, roads, other buildings, and so on.

Suppose you know you have water mains, gas pipelines, or other buried utilities that aren't connected with your project but simply transit through your property. In that case, you will need to hire a utility location company to help you with any of this.

Although special ground marking paint may be used in some situations, using wooden stakes is typically the better option. To get a better visual of larger areas, link them with string.

You'll know exactly where you need to work on the following steps once you've marked out your building site.

Clearing and Grubbing

After that, clear the designated areas of foliage, debris, and obstacles. This involves clearing trees, bushes, rocks, junk, roots, and anything else in your way.

You can hire a contractor to do it, but you should do it yourself if you want to save money. The more densely vegetated your area is, the more work it will be, and the more useful heavy machinery will be.

You must also consider what you will do with anything you accumulate. The vegetation could be broken up, with the small pieces being composted and the larger pieces used as firewood. Alternatively, you might simply pile it up and burn, bury, or haul it away.

The rest of the garbage would most likely need to be collected and hauled to a dumpsite. You could pay someone to pick it up and dump it for you if you don't have access to a vehicle.

Grading, Cut, and Fill

Once you've cleared everything out of the way on your building site, you will start to see what you have to deal with. An uneven building site can be acceptable depending on the base you choose, as long as a crane can drop the containers onto it from a nearby location. However, if you want a slab or perimeter base, you'll need to grade and build a level building pad.

Now is also a perfect time to go over the drainage planning you did earlier. You may need to install swales and berms to regulate water flow, protect your container home, and divert water away from it.

You'll also need to make improvements to your access road. According to the discussion above, you should have chosen a route ideal for you and any contractors, but you might still need some surface prep work to smooth bumps and minimize steep grades. You may also need to build bridges, concrete low-water crossings, or culverts at any place where water flows.

Road Building

Road building is closely related to the last part of the previous segment. Although a road cut through the existing soil might be appropriate in certain circumstances, it is usually preferable to cover it with dirt, road base, asphalt, or even concrete to create a more stable, all-weather surface.

You may be able to wait, but keep in mind that heavy equipment trucks can seriously damage a dirt road, requiring you to return and regrade it later.

Erosion Control

The previous steps involved removing vegetation and moving dirt, all of which are ideal conditions for erosion.

Rain-induced erosion can cause unwanted sediment deposits on neighboring properties, sedimentation in ponds and streams, and loss of high-quality topsoil in the areas you cleared.

Planting an appropriate species of vegetation near the edge of where you cleared might be beneficial. Still, you'll need to leave the directly cleared areas bare in preparation for future construction activities.

As a result, temporary erosion control devices such as wattles, blankets, and silt fences must be used. These products won't stop erosion entirely, but they will keep them contained throughout the construction process.

Any of these options may be needed by law as part of a Storm Water Pollution Prevention Plan (SWPPP) or other similar planning documents, depending on your area. More details should be available from the Environmental Quality office in your state or region.

Fencing and Security

Your project is progressing at this point, and you've most likely begun to spend money. You might also have tools and supplies that you'd like to leave on the worksite when you're not working.

Our discussion of container locks and security is a good read on some ways to protect your container and the area around it.

Since you are unlikely to have your containers on-site at this time, not all of the recommendations in that section would apply to you.

For now, we suggest putting up a fence around the property. Now is an excellent time to build one if you intend to do so anyway. You can save money by clearing a fence line while you have the equipment on hand to clear the building site.

If a fence isn't feasible financially, a security camera or lighting can suffice. Your requirements are largely determined by the things you need to safeguard and the location of your house.

Planning for and Installing Utilities

Getting utilities to your construction site is critical for helping you live in your container home and making the building process go more smoothly. Without utilities, you will have to rely on water tanks, generators, and port-a-potties.

Although you'll usually have to contact each company separately, tools like in My Area will show you which companies (across several utility types) service your location.

Check to see if all of the utilities have a monthly minimum fee. If that's the case, we suggest waiting to do the hookup until you are ready to begin construction. Doing it early would only result in you paying the minimum bill, regardless of whether you use it.

Some services may be deregulated, essentially monopolized by one company, or government-controlled, depending on where you live. If you choose as a customer between several companies that offer the same utility service, do some research to see which one is the better fit for your needs.

You can also see if they have any energy savings bonuses or rebates that you might qualify for with only a few changes to your design. Utilities can offer financial incentives to use better insulation and windows, as well as energy-efficient appliances, among other things. Be sure to ask!

Electricity

Electricity is the first and, arguably, most significant utility. Contact the nearest electrical cooperative or company to learn more about installing an electric meter and connecting to the power grid.

You should get electrical service installed if there are power lines on the main road near your house. The cost will be determined by factors such as whether a new transformer is required, the duration (and difficulty) of the run, and whether it will be run underground or on poles.

Typically, the company will have a set distance of wire and poles/trenching, beyond which you will be charged for every additional distance. They should be able to provide you with an estimate. Understand that they are also giving you a discount on the actual installation cost with the expectation that they will benefit from your monthly service charge over time.

As a result, another issue you may face is the electrical company's desire to see some kind of improvement in your construction before committing to providing electrical service to your site. If they are unsure that you can finish the container home and become a loyal client, they will be hesitant to pay for the installation. Alternatively, they can encourage you to pay for a larger share of the cost yourself to minimize the risk. Each company is different, so find out what the requirements are in your area.

Understand that permits and approvals may be needed, especially with additional overhead poles that may affect neighbors. According to our previous point about minimum charges, you don't have to start the installation right away, but you can contact them as soon as possible to learn about the process and timeline.

You'll probably want to have temporary power installed first, which will provide you with a few electrical circuits as part of the operation. It should be enough for the building, but it is insufficient for the entire house. The company will return after the house is completed to install your permanent service.

Suppose commercial electric service isn't cost-effective, going off the grid with a generator. In that case, solar panels or wind turbines could be a better option than paying the electric company to extend service to you.

Gas

Gas is good for space heating, water heaters, and stoves and includes natural gas or propane, a slightly less common alternative, propane. If you're in the city, you could have access to a natural gas line that you can tap into with a meter, similar to how electrical service is provided.

In more rural areas, you can normally rent or buy a big tank that stores gas which can last for months.

It is best to find out gas prices in your region so you can make decisions about the appliances you want to use in your home. However, if gas is available, it is the most cost-effective and easiest to use.

Sewer and Septic

If your property has connections to nearby sewage lines, you'll need to determine how much it will cost and how long it will take to link. A septic system is likely your only choice in more rural areas.

A septic system would typically cost more to install than a sewer connection. Still, it will cost virtually nothing to use and maintain after the installation compared to the monthly fee associated with your sewer connection.

A buried tank or tanks and a buried line with leach pipes or sprinklers are standard features of most septic systems. Work with your installer to develop a suitable place for this equipment that will not obstruct potential development or livability.

Telecommunications

Although some people build shipping container houses in rural areas to get away from it all, most people prefer having some connectivity. The choices available vary greatly depending on your location.

You could have many options in the city, including cable, DSL, and fiber, which combine internet, television, and even phone service into a single bill. To get these services outside of the area, you may have to rely on satellite dishes, slower cable connections, or even point-to-point terrestrial radio frequency technology.

If you have many options, make sure you call around, compare rates, and do some haggling. We'd also suggest talking to your neighbors to see what kind of approach they use and how they like it.

Early telecommunication access can be beneficial for tying in security camera surveillance, for example, and allowing fast Google searches or online shopping right from the building site!

Water

Water is last but not least. In the United States, the same water you use to bathe is also the water you drink, while in other nations, you'll need to buy potable bottled water separately.

In any case, all but the most remote areas have access to a water source. If you can't get access for a reasonable price, you'll have to either dig a well or pay to get water trucked in and stored in a tank on site.

These solutions have higher initial costs, but they can be very affordable if you plan on keeping your container home for a long time.

This in-depth discussion of required site planning activities should be a key step in designing and constructing a container home. Paying attention to this area would help you save money and transform a good home into a great home.

CHAPTER 4: PLANNING

How To Plan Your Shipping Container Home

Planning is essential for any project, and shipping container homes are no exception.

The typical new home project goes over budget and time by around 20 percent. You must create and adhere to a solid plan.

Let's take a closer look at how to schedule the design of your shipping container home correctly.

Set Your Budget

Setting a budget is the first step in building a house.

It's pointless to decide to create a 4,000-square-foot house if you only have $50,000 to work with.

Determine how much money you have in your account. If you can borrow money from a bank or a family member, the amount would be added to the amount of money you have available for the project. This is your budget.

Have a 20% contingency fund. A contingency fund is a set of funds set aside to cover unforeseen costs that might arise during the construction of your house. The majority of construction projects have unforeseen costs.

With total cash available of $150,000, this is how the contingency fund is measured. 20% of $150,000 = $30,000. Subtract the $30,000 contingency sum from your total available fund of $150,000. This leaves you with the actual budget for building your container house. Your construction budget is now $120,000, plus a $30,000 contingency budget. Your project must be focused on that $120,000 amount, with $30,000 set aside for any problems that might occur.

Decide and Finalize Your Design

It's now time to start planning your shipping container house. By the way, you can figure out your budget before moving on to this stage so that you can prepare realistically.

You can design anything, from a single container tiny house to a multi-story mansion! The possibilities for shipping container combinations are virtually infinite, and they can be tailored to your exact specifications.

The best way to plan is to start with the logical questions before getting bogged down in the details, such as how many containers do I need, how do I insulate my house, and so on.

Instead, consider things like what the building will be used for, how many people will use it, and so on. Take it one step at a time. Make the most important decisions first. Then, as you go along, add more info. Keep in mind that the more precise your responses, the better your design will be.

Changing your mind about a design halfway through construction costs a lot of money. Don't make the same mistake as the couple who wanted to remove a container's internal wall. They then decided they didn't want the open-plan room after all and reinstalled the wall. They lost $5,000 in material and time as a result of the changes.

This cost could have been avoided with better planning!

Decide Who Will Build It

Once you've settled on a concept for your shipping container home, you'll need to consider who will build it.

Many people choose to make their shipping container structures. This is a more cost-effective and rewarding option. If you want to construct a shipping container home yourself, consider using sufficiently appropriate experience and practical skills.

If you don't have the necessary skills or time, you should consider hiring a contractor to build your home for you.

Contractors are usually more experienced and can complete the project in less time. They would, however, be costly. If you're considering hiring a contractor, ensure you:

• Ask for references.

• Do they guarantee their work?

• How long does the guarantee last?

• Do they have liability insurance?

Where Will You Build Your Shipping Container Home?

You've agreed on a budget, a design for your container house, and who will build it. It's now time to look for a piece of land that suits your needs.

I advise people to design their container homes before they look for land to design the exact shipping container home they want rather than one that is limited by a specific piece of land.

Choose a specific area where you want to develop before looking for a plot of land. You can search for land online using sites like Zillow, or you can do it the old-fashioned way by driving around. You can sometimes get an absolute bargain!

Don't undervalue the importance of driving around the place you've chosen. Look for any signs that say "for sale." Speak with the people who live there. Locals may be aware of land available for purchase before it appears on the real estate market.

Once you've found a piece of land you like, make an appointment to meet with the local zoning/planning department. You must speak with them to determine whether or not they are willing to issue you a building permit to construct a shipping container home in their jurisdiction. If the local planning department is adamantly opposed to the idea, it may be better to find a plot of land in a different district.

Is Your Shipping Container Home Feasible?

Do you have the necessary skills and tools to build a shipping container home? Building a shipping container home is time-consuming and expensive, and it necessitates a wide range of skills.

Time and money are the two most valuable resources you would need. Then you'll need either the DIY know-how and ability to turn the shipping container into a home or the financial means to employ someone to do it for you.

Before you begin construction, you should think about where you would get your building materials. For example, if you want to construct a shipping container home but live 1,000 miles away from the nearest container depot, it will not be feasible. Getting your containers shipped over such a distance will cost you a lot of money and take a long time.

Building permits/planning approval is the last important factor to consider. It's a sad fact, but you won't be able to get a building permit to build a shipping container home in certain parts of the world. If this is the stance of your local planning department, then you'll have a hard time persuading them to change their minds

It's often easier to construct a container home in a different district with different zoning and planning regulations!

You should now be able to plan your new shipping container home, from budgeting to finding a plot of land.

CHAPTER 5: GREAT IDEAS FOR SHIPPING CONTAINERS

When you think about shipping containers, you typically think of massive steel boxes used to transport vast quantities of hazardous goods and other products from one location to another. While it was their main purpose in the past, it is no longer the case. Nowadays, shipping containers are being used for a variety of structures.

People began using shipping containers for their homes about a decade ago to save money and enjoy a low-maintenance lifestyle. Furthermore, shipping containers are a more environmentally friendly alternative to regular housing, so everyone wins.

But there's more to shipping containers than meets the eye. Countries worldwide follow suit, using these multipurpose rectangular boxes for structures ranging from hotels to movie theaters to shopping malls.

Why should a company keep a shipping container when it is no longer needed? Here are a few ideas:

Unique uses for shipping containers

1. School. Building a school is quite expensive; although it is costly to construct a school, education is still required for the world's children. So, how do you go about it? Shipping containers have been used in schools in third-world countries and other underprivileged areas worldwide, which is a fantastic way to save money. Furthermore, many of these classrooms are equipped with solar panels, allowing them to save electricity.

2. Hotel. Many people live in shipping containers, so it's only logical that they can also be utilized as hotels. Many countries around the world have turned these containers into hotels. Some are permanent, while others may be moved to different places.

3. Bridge A proposed project in Israel will transform decommissioned shipping containers into a 525-foot-long bridge. Space was once a landfill; however, it is now an open park that leads to Ariel Sharon National Park.

4. Clinic or hospital. Can't you get to the hospital? Let it come to you. Containers can be utilized to establish mobile clinics, allowing more people to receive medical care. These clinics can also be made permanent and affixed to a fixed location.

5. Furniture. Shipping containers can be turned into long-lasting furniture for homeowners and schools. Whether you're looking to create chairs, tables, or desks, you can't get much sturdier than shipping container material.

6. Portable toilet. Containers make excellent toilets for building sites. These can be found in various countries, and because of their portability, they can easily be moved from one project to another.

7. Movie theater. Although shipping containers can only serve as a

temporary movie theater, they can provide a lot of recreational value in a short period.

8. Stores. It's not rare to see stores – even entire malls – constructed out of shipping containers in countries outside the United States.

9. Food truck. Using shipping containers, you may keep your food truck in one spot rather than traveling from one location to another. You can modify a shipping container such that the roof and sides "pop out," resulting in a unique work of art that showcases your creativity. This concept is also applicable to small shops.

10. Coffee bars and cafes. Create your café and coffee bar out of a shipping container to save money on commercial space.

11. Student housing. Shipping containers are used for student accommodation in other countries. These containers are stacked and used as dorms at several colleges and universities.

12. Barn. Because of their many useful properties, shipping containers are a natural choice for barns. They are fire-resistant.

Shipping containers are also wind and water-tight, so they are a must-have if you reside in a region with severe weather conditions.

13. Playhouse. Keep your children occupied/entertained with a shipping container playhouse. A shipping container playhouse will keep your youngsters occupied. You can set it up however you like. It can be made large or small and painted in any color you like. Add games and television; the playhouse will be ideal for sleepovers with friends.

14. Playground. Because shipping containers are designed to be stacked, you may construct a unique playground for the kids by making minor alterations and adding some pipes as slides.

15. Office or Workshop. You may not have enough space to work on projects at home due to limited space. Containers make great workshops and cubicles. With a few tweaks, you can install windows and doors to create a private space where you can concentrate on your job.

16. Patio or deck. While wood is commonly used for decks, bees and other critters are known to wreak havoc. You can avoid this problem by utilizing a container. Create some open space or add some windows to your patio, and you will have a unique space.

17. Garden. A shipping container garden is ideal for growing plants and foods for deer and others. Put windows on all sides so that the sun can shine in and the plants can grow to their full potential. This type of garden is simple to manage, and the added protection ensures that your hard work and time aren't wasted.

18. Pool. You can make your pool by burying a container underground. With a few little tweaks, you'll have something to keep you cool this summer. Containers range in length from 10-53 feet, so you can stack as many as you need to get the size you want. Creating your shipping container pool allows you to get creative and add paint, wood, and other decorative features to suit your

tastes.

19. Sauna. If a pool isn't relaxing enough, what about your sauna? Containers also make great saunas.

Shipping containers are ideal for various structures and are particularly useful in impoverished areas where constructing something from scratch would be prohibitively expensive. These are just a few examples of how containers have worked well in the past. Using your imagination, you can probably think of a lot more uses for these strong steel boxes.

SIMPLE STEPS TO BUILDING YOUR SHIPPING CONTAINER

Building a house isn't easy, and while shipping containers make the process go faster, it still requires a lot of effort and planning. To make things easier, we've put up this guide to get you started on your journey to domestic happiness in your very own shipping container home.

Here is what you need to know before starting a shipping container home project.

How to build your shipping container home

1) Sort out permits, planning, and compliance

This is one area where cutting corners is not an option. To verify that you are permitted to build a home and that one made out of shipping containers fits with local and district plans, you will need to obtain all necessary permits and planning permission from the local council. Working with your architects and structural engineer to ensure that your proposed shipping container building is structurally sound is also required. Find an architect who has worked with shipping containers before, as building with them is very different from building with wood, brick, or steel.

2) Acquire your shipping containers

Once your initial plans have been approved, You'll need to get your shipping containers. The scope of your plans will determine the size and amount of shipping containers you'll need. You can ensure that you get the greatest quality and grade of containers for the best price by Speaking with the sales team at Gateway Container Sales & Hire. It's at this point that you'll have to select whether you'll buy your containers already modified from the supplier's workshop or if you'll make your container alterations. While it may appear to be cheaper to do it yourself at first, it may be far easier in the long run to have the containers modified and cut by specialists to ensure that they are structurally solid and to speed up the job.

3) Hire a project manager, subcontractors, and builders

What sort of team you'll need depends on your level of building skill and experience, as well as the amount of time you have available. Some people may regard themselves to be the typical Aussie bloke, capable of doing everything themselves. We've all seen the DIY nightmare shows on TV, and we recommend that if you want a professional outcome, you should get some professional aid, especially if this is your first time working with shipping containers as a construction material or if the job is enormous.

Most housing projects require a project manager, a team of builders, electricians, gas fitters, plumbers, glaziers, gib stoppers, painters, and plasterers. Before you invest your hard-earned money, having them build your container dream home, shop around and make sure you have qualified tradies with a solid reputation and plenty of previous work to look at. Cutting corners now could cost you later, so do it well the first time so you can be proud of your container home.

4) Prepare the site

You'll have to get the building site ready for construction. This will involve any necessary earthworks and various utilities such as power, gas lines, stormwater drains, septic tanks, sewerage, and plumbing.

5) Lay the foundations for your shipping container home

The requirements for your shipping container home foundations will be determined by several factors, including the building site conditions, climate, local market design, overall building design, and construction costs. Utilities will be installed according to the plans, and a concrete slab will be poured.

6) Modify the containers

This step will depend on whether you plan to modify/customize the containers yourself to modify them when you buy them. It's crucial to note that shipping container walls and roofs contribute to the container's and building's structural integrity, so get any container alterations approved by a structural engineer before cutting anything. Steel framing will be needed if the paneling is removed, and larger openings may require more reinforcement and support. All of the doors, windows, and other openings will be constructed at this time, and all joins should be weatherproofed.

7) Attach the containers to the foundations and each other

Now comes the fun part: moving your shipping containers on-site and into position on your foundations with a huge crane, hiab, etc. The strength and ability to stack shipping containers on top of each other make them so appealing. Place the containers according to the designs you approved before they were built, then connect them at the corners' attaching points. This can be made easier by laying steel plates in the foundation as the slab settles, then welding the containers to them to keep them in place.

8) Install exterior doors, windows, skylights, and ventilation

The vast majority of your building is up, and it probably went up in no time, thanks to the lego-like modular architecture of shipping containers. Installing all of your glass windows, skylights, doors, and ventilation is the next step in "sealing" the building. Remember to reinforce every window and door openings to ensure the building's structural integrity.

9) Install fixtures and fittings

Install insulation all through the building, and all electrical wiring, plumbing, and gas run through the foundations. Plaster the seams, install drywall or GIB plasterboard, and paint the interior of the building. By now, you should have completed 99 percent of your shipping container home, and it's time to add the finishing touches. It's also time to put the kitchen and bathrooms in place.

10) Inspection and sign off

Hopefully, at this point, everything has been completed correctly, and your building is ready for inspection. Cross your fingers and schedule an inspection to make sure your building is up to code. This is your last chance to make major adjustments to the shipping container structure.

11) Landscaping and decorating

Your container home should be done, signed off, and ready to move in by now, but there are still some finishing touches to be made. It's time to landscape the region so that your structure blends in with its natural surroundings, whether you're in the forest, city, desert, or anywhere else. It's also time to lay floor coverings, paint the interior, and make your new container house a liveable home.

Move-in and enjoy!

CHAPTER 6: HOW TO GET A SHIPPING CONTAINER

Steel shipping containers are a fun, easy, and affordable way to build a sturdy, portable structure in your yard, on your flatbed trailer, or at your business. You can also stack them (8+ high at sea during hurricanes), transport them cheaply, and use them to make an instant rooftop deck.

Metal shipping containers, like other industrial residues, can be difficult to locate and transport. This chapter will help you find containers for sale and obtain one — or ten.

Step 1: Research Regulations

If you are going to go through the trouble of putting a metal box in your yard that weighs several thousand pounds, make sure your local code enforcers aren't going to make you move it right away.

I am currently based in Austin, Texas. Because codes differ significantly from one location to the next, you'll need to double-check what the deal is in your specific neighborhood.

"Building detached one-story accessory structures with a floor space of less than 200 square feet (18.58 m2). Remember that you must follow all zoning rules and regulations regarding height, setbacks, and trade permits, even if you don't need a permit to build or install the structure. If you want to add plumbing or electricity to the structure, you'll need to get the appropriate trade permits.

Step 2: Decide Which Container You Want

There are various container styles and sizes to choose from.

20' length, 8' width, and 8.5' height. weighs 5,000 lbs.

40' long, 8' broad, and typically 8.5' tall. Weighs 8,000 lbs.

Other sizes, particularly other heights, are available, although they are by far the most common and often the most affordable per cubic foot.

A'refrigerated' option is available in both sizes. While it may seem appealing to save yourself the effort of insulating afterward, they cost thousands more, and I felt it was not worth it.

Step 3: Plan Your Layout

You can start planning how/where you'll use it once you know what size you're working with.

Sketchup is a good tool for this because it's free, integrates with Google Earth, and already has a shipping container model that you can modify.

Step 4: Find Your Container

There is the easy way, the hard way, and two tricks:

The easy way: Google "shipping containers for sale" and purchase one via a nationwide broker, eBay, or a local reseller. Expect to pay at least $2300+ for a 40', and $1,900+ for a 20'.

Hard way: figure out how to
purchase damaged/abandoned containers from a shipyard directly. I looked into it for a while but gave up after learning that a commercial driver's license would be required.

Trick #1: Instead of a shipping container, search for conex on craigslist. This is another term for it. Like the guy I purchased mine from, some container sellers show up if you search for conex but won't if you search for shipping container.

Trick #2: if purchasing from a dealer, make it clear that you do not need a cargo-worthy container, just one that is watertight. Cargo-worthy mainly refers to whether the metal channels on the bottom are straight to within an inch or not; this is vital for container-moving gear but probably won't be an issue for you. I was quoted prices $300+ more before I realized this.

Some places also provide a rent-to-own option, but it will cost you a lot of money. The cheapest I could find was nearly 20% off, and they might not be happy to find you customizing their container before you pay for it.

In mid-2010, I spent $1,300 for my 20'x8'x8.5' container, including delivery to my East Austin yard, and I think that was a great deal.

Prices are so low in the United States because of our trade deficit: we export significantly less than we import, and returning an empty container is expensive. These prices, of course, fluctuate with the price of the steel they're made of.

BUYING THE CONTAINERS

Tips You Need To Know Before Building A Shipping Container Home

One of the niche trends in sustainable design of the past few years has been the re-use of shipping containers to create the structure of a building. Shipping containers are well-suited for use in houses due to their compact size, and their appeal stems from their obvious simplicity: you get a room shipped in one piece, and you can stack them together to make multiple rooms or tie them together with larger rooms.

But, of course, nothing is ever as simple as it seems, and using shipping containers to build a home is still fraught with difficulties - particularly since the concept is still relatively new. Few people have the experience needed to construct one without a hitch. That's why we have enlisted the help of 23 experts worldwide - designers and owners who have faced obstacles to create their own container homes - to find out what they wish they had learned before taking on the project. Check out their 11 top tips.

1. Examine the containers you're purchasing " "I wish I hadn't bought my containers without seeing them first; I trusted the company's word that they would be in good condition. They were all beaten to a pulp."

2. Invest a little more in a one-trip container.

"I wish I had known that a One-Trip container isn't that expensive and is like brand new."

3. Familiarize yourself with the local rules in your area.

"Every country has its set of rules and regulations. This means that a container house in the United States is not the same as a container house in Denmark. That is something that most people do not consider. Although the container is a generic commodity, environment, fire regulations, and other factors are not..."

4. Find A Contractor That Can Do It All

"The one thing we would have done better is to find a single contractor to assist us in the process rather than hiring one for obtaining and changing the containers and another for finishing out the interior."

5. Understand the Shipping Container Market

"I wish I knew there were containers that are taller than 8 feet."

- Mark Wellen, Rhotenberry Wellen Architects

6. Understand The Shipping Container's Structure

"I think it's crucial to consider how their structural integrity works—for example, the two long walls are both load-bearing and bracing, so if you cut a hole in one, you'd have to compensate."

7. Do not Expect To Make A Huge Saving

"What I wish I had known that building a house out of shipping containers costs about the same as building a house out of sticks."

8. Minimize The Required Welding

"Welding takes a long time and is costly, so try to avoid it as much as possible."

9. Know How To Insulate

"I wish I had known how to insulate a shipping container; we ended up soldering elements on the walls and then spraying them with anti-fire foam insulation."

"We wish we'd known that in cold countries, you must ensure that you have enough insulation to avoid condensation."

10. Plan Ahead For Plumbing

"Having all of the plumbing chases cut out of the container floors and ceilings to conveniently run pipe until they were stacked would have made a significant difference."

11. Have A Strategy To Cope With Wind

"We weren't expecting too much wind on-site, and we now have to block it out with vegetation because the container makes a lot of noise when there are strong winds."

CHAPTER 7: INSULATION

What is Insulation?

Would you air-condition an open-air porch or patio that becomes too hot in the summer? Not without enclosing it by building walls first, of course!

Separate the conditioned air (air that has been artificially cooled or warmed, depending on the season) from the outside air. Otherwise, you are air conditioning the neighborhood.

If you built the walls around your porch out of plastic food wrap or newspaper, they would not be effective at regulating the temperate (even though they would keep the air separated). Why not?

A thin wall will not effectively prevent heat transmission from the heated to the cool side. While actual air cannot pass through the wall, the heat contained in the air can. So, despite the separation of the air, your energy efficiency would be rather low.

As a result, insulation is a material designed to keep heat from passing through the walls (and floor and ceiling) of your shipping container home. It works by trapping air or other gasses in a complex matrix of passages or tiny cells.

Gases conduct thermal energy poorly compared to solids and liquids, making them good insulators. The role of convection inside the gas is reduced by restricting the gases to millions of tiny cells, further increasing the material's insulating properties.

When we talk about thermal insulation, we almost always refer to conductive (and to a lesser extent, convective) heat flow. An "R-value" is used to measure the resistance to heat flow, which is also how insulation is rated (higher is better). Heat flow via radiation also has a role, as explained below.

Why do you need container home insulation?

When you insulate a shipping container, you are separating the conditioned airspace from the outside environment. It's the same procedure you'd use in practically any enclosed construction with climate control. As previously said, insulating material prevents heat from traveling from the warmer to the cooler side. This improves your container home's energy efficiency by minimizing the energy required to maintain the internal temperature.

Unlike some other types of residential buildings, shipping container homes feature a steel exterior. Steel is particularly ineffective at keeping your airspace at a different temperature than the air outside, given how good it is at conducting heat energy. As a result, shipping container homes require more insulation than other types of construction.

And don't forget that the steel of a container home may absorb a lot of radiant energy from the sun in the summer, making it hotter than the ambient air. Simply stated, unaltered shipping containers are excellent at keeping the outside air out. They do, however, a poor job of preventing heat from passing through their walls.

However, just because container homes are poor at preventing heat transmission doesn't mean you need to insulate them. Another factor to consider is the climate.

How climate affects your insulation decision

You might not need insulation material for your shipping container if you are lucky (or easygoing!) enough to reside in a climate that allows you to live comfortably without additional cooling or heating. Many people believe southern California and parts of the Mediterranean to have the perfect climate.

However, some people still require heating and air conditioning in these climates and should strongly consider insulation. Whether you need climate control in your shipping container home or not is a matter of personal preference for what is considered 'comfortable.' You might be able to tolerate normal temperatures without any added insulating material if you use fans in hot climates and warm clothes in colder ones.

If you do not reside in such a region, we strongly advise you to insulate your storage containers, but you don't HAVE to. You'd have to compare the cost of insulation (a one-time expense) against the continuous expenditures of running your air conditioner and heater.

You may also need a larger heater or air conditioner than you would if your container had insulated your container. Any money saved from not insulating quickly vanishes as the energy cost to keep the climate in your shipping container rises.

To summarize, you will almost certainly need to insulate your cargo container unless you reside in the ideal climate. And if you decide to go without insulation, you may come to regret it due to the additional money you'll have to spend on heating and cooling. The advantages of an insulated shipping container will be appreciated far more often than not.

One note of caution: if you do not insulate your container, your home will not only be difficult to heat and cool, but it will also be more subject to water condensation, which can cause corrosion and mold.

Where should your container insulation be placed?

The walls of most building types comprise multiple layers of materials. The material you see on the inside is not the same as what you see on the outside. Several layers of materials provide fire resistance, structure, weatherproofing, vapor barrier, thermal insulation, etc.

With shipping container homes, the container itself is one such layer.   In addition, you must decide where the container skin will be placed inside the overall wall system.

The most common solution is to install insulation within the shipping container's interior walls. Most designs have stud walls to run plumbing and electrical service and a point of attachment for drywall or other interior surfaces. It's simply common sense to insulate the spaces between the studs. Then, if you like, you can leave the container's exterior as you want.

However, outside insulation may be a better option for some folks. In this case, you'll need to put insulation outside the container and then cover it with weather-resistant sheathing. This provides increased interior space and a more controlled exterior appearance for people who prefer to hide or shield the shipping containers themselves.

Factors to consider when choosing shipping container insulation

Choosing the appropriate insulation for your home is more difficult than you think. Each type has advantages and disadvantages that may or may not be relevant to the specific conditions of your shipping containers.

As we go over each type of insulation, we'll try our best to provide a high-level description of some of these factors. However, bear in mind that prices may vary by region and manufacturer, so always conduct your research.

Things to consider when evaluating your insulation options include:

Overall Performance: The performance characteristics are influenced by entrapped gas, material, open vs. closed-cell structure, etc.

R-value: How well a material prevents heat energy transmission for a particular thickness.

Air Leakage: The effectiveness with which the insulation keeps air from passing through it (which has already been discussed, is a separate but related issue from blocking heat transfer)

Vapor Permeability: How well the insulation prevents vapor from passing through it and staying in it.

Cost: Factor in labor/equipment costs and material costs depending on whether you hire a contractor or do it yourself. If you are doing it yourself, remember the ease of installation and required tools are worth considering.

Many people are drawn to shipping container homes because they want to live in a sustainable, environmentally friendly manner.   The environmental impact of these materials varies a lot depending on how they're made and installed.

Types of Shipping Container Insulation

We'll go over five different types of insulation, all of which are classified by the physical form they take, which is directly tied to how they're applied. Much like peanuts and peanut butter might fall into two different food categories (or apples and applesauce, or... we'll just stop there!), some insulating materials, such as polyurethane foam and cellulose, may fall into more than one of the categories below if they may be purchased and installed in different ways.

Recognizing the distinctions between materials and evaluating how they affect your circumstances is the most crucial component of selecting the appropriate type of insulation for your situation. With that said, let's take a look at the various alternatives!

Non-traditional Insulation

This type of insulation is made up of unusual materials that are generally chosen at least in part for their environmental friendliness and are commonly referred to as "cheap" insulation. Because of their low R-value per inch, they are less ideal for most owners unless eco-friendliness is your priority and you are willing to sacrifice interior space for it.

While they are cost-effective forms of insulation, their applicability is often limited. They may be ideal for more temperate climates with less extreme temperature variations.

Straw Bale: A straw bale stacked like blocks, similar to the kind you'd use to feed a horse. Because of the size of straw bales, this would only work for container insulation on the outside.

Hempcrete: Hempcrete is a material made of hemp that is similar to concrete but with less strength.

Blanket Insulation

Blanket insulation comes in the form of batts (pre-cut lengths to meet normal wall heights) and rolls (large rolled-up pieces that must be cut to length during installation). It's "fluffy," compressible, and not self-supporting. It's similar to a blanket you'd use to keep warm in your house on a cold winter evening, but it's thicker and made of different materials. Blanket insulation is nearly always made up of long fibers mashed together in a small space, thus making it open-celled.

Blanket insulation is designed to be fastened in the cavities between studs. It relies on the studs for structural stiffness because it would otherwise collapse into a pile without support. It's the most affordable option and is simple to install, requiring only a stapler to fasten to studs.

Varieties of blanket insulation include:

Fiberglass Insulation: This is made of tiny fibers spun from superheated sand or recycled glass. This is the most common type of low-cost wall insulation in Western countries.

Mineral Wool, Slag Wool, and Rock Wool Insulation: Similar to fiberglass, but made from ceramics/minerals or 'slag,' a byproduct of metal production.

Sheep Wool Insulation: Sheep wool insulation is exactly what it sounds like insulation made from the sheared wool of sheep.

Denim or Cotton Insulation: It is often blueish tint because it is made from recycled denim or blue jeans. Expensive, but with a large percentage of recycled contents.

Blanket insulation is permeable to water vapor, which a vapor retarder in traditional construction can mitigate. On the other hand, Vapor retarders are usually not a smart choice for container houses since the outer metal layer is already a vapor barrier. By adding a second barrier, you risk trapping water vapor in the wall cavities.

Some blanket insulation fibers, most notably fiberglass, can irritate the eyes, skin, and respiratory systems. Before handling these materials, wear proper PPE (personal protective equipment) such as gloves, dust masks, and safety glasses. For proper handling procedures, consult the MSDS (Material Safety Data Sheet) or any instructions on the product packaging.

Loose-Fill Insulation

This type of insulation depends on applying small macroscopic (clearly visible with the naked eye) bits of insulating material are applied to a wall cavity. These insulators require complete wall cavity containment before application, or you'll end up with a pile on your floor.

Cellulose Insulation: is made from shredded recycled paper goods that are blown in by a machine.

Loose-Fill Fiberglass Insulation: Fiberglass insulation is similar to fiberglass batts, but it is not tightly bound, and it's less dense, allowing it to be blown in by a machine.

Perlite Insulation and Vermiculite Insulation: Minerals have been heated and expanded like popcorn, resulting in a natural foam pellet added to wall cavities.

Loose-fill insulating materials aren't suggested for containers because of their vapor permeability.

Expanded Foam Insulation

Expanded foam is pre-sized for normal wall heights and manufactured off-site into huge boards and insulation panels. These insulation panels, unlike blanket insulation, are self-supporting. Holes for things like windows and doors are made on-site by cutting. Similar to spray foam insulation, the gas in closed cell expanded foam variants can escape the cells, resulting in a lower R-value over time.

Expanded foam is DIY-friendly and can be attached directly to the container or fastened to studs. Unless you have a lot of cuts to make, it may be fairly rapid to install. Some are molded to look like the grooves of a shipping container wall. You will have large air gaps in these corrugated sections.

In most circumstances, expanded foam insulation offers the highest R-value per inch of all insulating materials.

Open Cell Polyurethane Foam Insulation: Open-cell foam cells aren't as dense and filled with air, giving insulation a lower R-value and a spongy texture.

Closed Cell Polyurethane Foam Insulation: The 'blowing agent' fills the tiny microscopic cells with a gas other than air that has greater heat conduction capabilities, raising the R-value of the foam.

Extruded Polystyrene Foam Insulation: It is a closed-cell foam made up of tiny plastic beads fused. It's the white foam you've probably seen in things like coffee cups.

Expanded Polystyrene Foam Insulation: Begins as a molten material pressed out of a form into closed-cell foam sheets. While the name is similar to EPS, it is not the same.

Polyisocyanurate: Similar to polyurethane but has more rigidity

Spray Insulation

Spray insulation comes in various materials, all of which are applied by pumping or spraying a liquid mixture that hardens into a solid. Spray insulation is continuous and expands into nooks, crannies, and gaps because it is applied and adheres to itself. This creates a barrier that prevents both air movement and heat transfer.

Spray foam insulation expands when it is applied and subsequently solidifies, aiding in the sealing process. However, because the foam will expand past the face of your studs, it will need to be trimmed.

Open-Cell Spray Polyurethane Foam: This is a less desirable type of polyurethane spray foam insulation because it allows air to travel between cells, resulting in a lower R-value per inch.

Closed-Cell Spray Polyurethane Foam: This is the most typical shipping container insulation, and it's what we recommend to most owners. This spray foam insulation has one of the highest R-values per inch and works well as a vapor retarder. Off-gassing after spray application is an issue, so check with your manufacturer for cure periods and how long you should wait before moving in. The gas in these closed-cell variations can occasionally escape the cells, resulting in a lower R-value over time.

Non-expanding sprayed-in insulation is a different but similar approach. Unlike the other spray foam insulation kinds, it does not chemically expand when applied, but it does move around to fill the space.

Damp-Spray Cellulose Insulation: This is made from shredded recycled paper products. Rather than using a standard blown-in application, a specific rig that adds water or adhesives at the site of application (known as damp-spraying) can be used to bind the cellulose together and allow it to be applied to open-sided wall cavities.

Cementitious Foam Insulation: A very light mixture of water, natural minerals, and air looks like concrete when cured but looks like shaving cream when applied and can be a bit crumbly after curing if not handled carefully. Thanks to its ingredients, cementitious foam is non-toxic, non-flammable, and eco-friendly, despite lagging spray foam insulation in R-value.

As you can see, there are a lot of options to choose from. Choosing the best insulation for you necessitates a thorough understanding of your decision-making factors, such as budget, design, climate, and tolerance to cold and heat.

If you're unsure what to do, look at what others in your area are already doing. Using materials that are common in your area is generally easier and less expensive. A conversation with a local contractor to gain site-specific advice and recommendations could also be useful.

Refrigerated Shipping Containers

Most of them are based on the idea of insulating a standard shipping container. There is, however, another option: buying an insulated shipping container that was formerly used to transport cold goods such as flowers and produce. This option has several advantages and disadvantages, but it can be a good choice to find these containers at a fair price.

Other Thermal Energy Control Ideas That Are Not Really "Insulation"

Green Roof

A green roof, also known as a living roof, is a rooftop garden made up of various grasses and other plants. Although soil and plants aren't great insulators, if you live in a warm environment, they can help block solar radiation. As a result, a green roof is more of a supplement than a replacement for more traditional forms of insulation.

Green roofs also have the added benefit of being appealing. From the sky, y Your container home will appear to be just another patch of ground. While it isn't the best option for insulation, it is still an environmentally friendly option that adds an element of protection.

Radiant/Reflective Barriers

While the other types of insulation discussed above help restrict the transmission of heat energy by conduction (and to a lesser degree, convection), we still have to consider radiation. Radiation is the least understood heat transfer method, but it is still incredibly significant in shipping container homes.

Unless you're willing to drape your container in a mylar space blanket like those typically carried by hikers, getting a radiation barrier is likely going to require some form of coating. Be careful to distinguish between paint and coatings that are meant to reflect and emit radiation energy.

Coatings are particularly formulated to reflect the invisible infrared light of thermal energy, and while they may look like paint, they function very differently.

Passive Heating and Cooling Design

Another approach is to design your home to use the least energy to heat and cool it. Several approaches can be used to do this. Examples include Solar Chimneys, Trombe Walls, and others. The efficiency of these strategies varies a lot depending on where you live.

These passive approaches can be effective in more moderate climates, although they are generally insufficient on their own. For example, in a passively designed container, the coolest you'll ever feel is if you're standing outside in the shade with a wind blowing. Even if that's too hot, a passive design won't suffice.

Making a Decision

A large number of options available when shipping container home insulation is a common theme running throughout this chapter, as you may have observed. But keep in mind that insulation is only one piece of a broader plan and building design.

Container home insulation should be considered in the context of your overall needs and architectural ideas. It must be taken into consideration from the beginning, as it affects practically every subsequent decision. It must also fit into your entire budget, considering factors such as climate, size of the structure, ease of installation, personal preference, and more.

We want to make sure you're satisfied with your shipping container house. Happiness, as the saying goes, is reality minus your expectations.

You will end up with a project you love if you understand the reality of financial resources and physics and how to manage your expectations for things like interior comfort. So get started as soon as possible and create a clear vision for your shipping container construction project.

Take the time you need to plan for the shipping container home that's best for you, and utilize this book to supplement any questions or concerns you may have as you journey.

You have a variety of insulation options to select from, and your decision is influenced by factors such as your design, climate, and budget. All options have advantages and disadvantages, but you now have a better knowledge of what those are.

It's important to keep in mind that you don't have to entirely utilize a specific type of insulation. For example, you could insulate the container walls and roof using closed-cell polyurethane spray foam insulation, then utilize rock wool blankets beneath the container to minimize cost.

Insulation can even be combined in the same area. For instance, you could use the rock wool underneath the container, then spray an inch of closed-cell polyurethane foam over the rock wool to create an airtight seal. Make sure you understand the implications of condensation if you are in a climate where condensation is a concern.

CHAPTER 8. UNDERSTAND HOW TO MANAGE CONDENSATION

If you've done any research on shipping container homes, you'll know that condensation is a common complaint. Container rain, container sweating, wall wetness, and other terms have been used to describe it. It's a technical subject that might be perplexing, but our goal is to lift the veil of mystery that surrounds it. This chapter will put you through how condensation forms, why it's a concern for shipping container homes, what the effects of condensation can be, and how to stop it.

It may appear tedious at first to learn all of the science of condensation, but we believe you must grasp the "why" behind the "what." There are companies out there willing to take your money for products that don't work, and there are people who mean well but incorrect advice. So let's begin by laying a solid foundation of knowledge, and then we'll go on to the effect and prevention of condensation.

What is condensation?

You've experienced condensation if you've ever seen early morning dew on your grass, watched water droplets form on the outside of a cold drinking glass, or discovered your bathroom mirror covered in "fog" after a hot shower.

Condensation is the transformation of water from a gaseous state (water vapor) to a liquid state (in the form of water droplets). A decrease in temperature causes this phase change, which usually occurs in the presence of a solid substrate onto which the droplets form (the grass, bathroom mirror, and drinking glass, in our examples).

When and how does condensation form?

You may have noticed that the conditions have to be right for condensation to form in our examples above. For example, there isn't always dew on your grass in the morning.

But what are these conditions? Keep your hat on because things are about to get technical! We'll look at psychrometrics, which is the science of studying the properties of gas-vapor mixtures.

To comprehend condensation, we must first comprehend humidity. When people talk about humidity, they usually mean 'relative humidity,' which is a percentage of the quantity of water vapor in a volume of air compared to the greatest amount of water vapor that could be in that same volume of air at that same temperature. Relative humidity of 30% indicates that the air contains 30% of the moisture that it might retain at that temperature.

Another measure of humidity is absolute humidity, which is the quantity of water in a given volume of air at a certain temperature and is generally expressed in grams per cubic meter (g/m3).

The amount of water vapor that air can contain increases as the temperature rises (in other words, relative humidity of 100% corresponds to a higher absolute humidity at higher temperatures). The relative humidity drops if the air temperature rises, but the moisture content remains constant). The opposite is also true: as the temperature of the airdrops, so does the amount of water vapor it can hold.

It's easy to comprehend with an example. Let's say we are at sea level, and the air is saturated with water vapor (meaning it has 100 percent relative humidity and is unable to hold any more moisture). When the temperature is 86 degrees Fahrenheit (30 degrees Celsius), the air contains around 28 grams of water per cubic meter. However, at 46°F (8°C), that air will only contain 8 grams of water per cubic meter (assuming we're still at 100 percent relative humidity).

Let's say we're back at sea level, with air at 86°F (30°C), but the relative humidity is only 50 percent (and the absolute humidity is roughly 15 g/m3). As the air temperature is reduced, the relative humidity rises above 50%, while the absolute humidity remains constant at 15 g/m3.

At some point, the temperature will have dropped low enough that the relative humidity will reach 100% (but the absolute humidity will remain at 15g/m3). This temperature is known as the dew point temperature. The temperature at which the air can hold the most water vapor (a state we previously defined as being saturated). The dew point temperature in our example is around 65°F (18°C).

What exactly does this imply? We'll have a problem if we lower the air temperature below 65°F (18°C). The capacity for water vapor in lower-temperature air is diminished, but the water vapor currently in the air needs to go somewhere. You are correct if you guessed that this excess water vapor turns into condensation.

Let's imagine we wish to lower the temperature to 50 degrees Fahrenheit (10 degrees Celsius) in our example. At this temperature and altitude, fully saturated (100 percent relative humidity) air has an absolute humidity of roughly 9.5g/m3.

But keep in mind that our cubic meter of air had 15g/m3 of water vapor when it reached the dewpoint of 65°F (18°C). This means that out of each cubic meter of air to reach 50°F (10°C), 5.5 grams of water vapor will have to condense!

Where does the condensation physically occur? On any object or surface with a temperature below the dewpoint.

After hours (or days) of exposure, practically all bathroom surfaces (floor, walls, mirror, sink, etc.) reach the same temperature as the internal air of your house. Water condenses on all of these cooler surfaces (below the dewpoint temperature) as the moist air from your hot shower (with approximately 100 percent relative humidity) contacts these cooler surfaces.

Unless you take a long, hot shower, you'll likely only notice condensation on the mirror because the water bends the light of your reflection and makes it quite easy to observe when compared to other surfaces. You won't get condensation on your mirror if you heat it. Alternatively, take a cold shower, and there will be no condensation in the bathroom!

What are the sources of moisture in a building?

It's critical to understand that condensation must be passed into a structure, usually by moisture-filled air. This can happen in a variety of ways, some of which you may not have considered:

Respiration (Breathing): Water vapor is included in your breath every time you exhale. The vapor will condense into the fog on cold days as it comes into contact with the cold air!

Sweating (perspiration): Sweating is the major cooling mechanism of the human body. Sweat turns into water vapor in the interior air when it evaporates.

Showers: We've already talked about how hot showers introduce air saturated with water vapor into a bathroom. That water vapor will remain inside the structure without proper ventilation.

Cooking: Many forms of cooking, particularly those involving boiling water, release water vapor into your kitchen. Like a bathroom, without proper ventilation, this water vapor remains inside the building.

Washing dishes: If you have ever opened a dishwasher after it's finished cleaning and been met with a face full of steam, you've experienced the humidity that a dishwasher can bring into an interior space.

Drying clothes: While washing clothes at a high temperature (or on a steam cycle) may introduce moisture into the interior area after opening the washer door, the more usual culprit is an incorrectly vented clothes dryer that does not send the moist air outside the structure. If you dry your clothes naturally on a rack, you'll have the same issue unless you do it outside the building.

Ironing clothes: It should come as no surprise that when a clothes iron is set to steam, water vapor is released into the air of your space.

Non-electric space heaters: Oil-fired, propane space heaters and gas (as well as wood stoves with inadequately seasoned wood) release moisture during the combustion process, which can enter into your home if not properly vented out through the flue.

Damp building materials: During construction, 'green' wood or other materials exposed to rain or other precipitation can release moisture into the air. If you close in your materials during part of the construction process, you risk trapping moist materials behind your walls, where they can cause problems.

Improper external liquid water sealing: Melting snow and ice, groundwater, rain, and surface runoff can bring liquid water into your building if wall and roof seams and penetrations are not properly sealed.

Plumbing leaks: Pinholes in pipes, as well as leaking fittings and connections, can allow water into your home, typically in places that are difficult to reach or see.

Pressure Differentials: When parts of your house are under negative pressure compared to the outside environment, outside air can be drawn into the structure through open doors and windows or air leakage through smaller gaps. If the outside air is humid and warm, this can introduce moisture into the structure.

It's worth noting that several of the most moisture-producing activities are associated with three sections of your home: the bathroom, kitchen, and laundry. While this is not the norm in most western construction, in most countries, in many countries, it is common to see all three (3) of those located outside of the conditioned (heated and cooled) sections of the house. This prevents the majority of moisture from entering the house in the first place, as well as reducing the amount of floor space you'll have to heat and cool.

The disadvantage of this strategy is that you'll be cooking, bathing, and cleaning outside, so you might need a fan or a coat depending on where you live. It's not an option for every container home project. Still, it's worth exploring because you're already breaking the mold of a traditional building by employing shipping containers in the first place!

As you can see from our list, moisture can enter and exit your structure in various ways. Almost every source applies to any construction, not simply shipping container construction. So, what is it about containers that cause condensation to be such a widely discussed issue?

Why is condensation so crucial to consider when constructing a shipping container home?

Condensation isn't specific to shipping containers, although all-metal structures have specific characteristics that make condensation more of a worry than in traditional construction:

Air Leakage: Traditional construction can be prone to air leaks due to the number of individual pieces used, gaps between pieces that arise when craftsmanship is less than optimal, incorrect sealing around penetrations, and other factors. In contrast, many metal buildings (particularly shipping containers) tend to be more firmly sealed, with less inadvertent ventilation. While this has certain advantages, such as weather and pest resistance, it can also mean that moist air inside is less likely to escape out. Moisture can be trapped indoors if you aren't proactive.

Permeability: Permeability is a measure of the ability of a porous material to allow fluids (liquids and gases) to move into and through it. More porous materials (such as sheathing, wooden studs, and so on) are used in traditionally constructed structures to safely absorb (and later release) moisture before condensation occurs. On the other hand, metal buildings are nearly entirely made of non-permeable materials like steel (except for insulation), allowing apparent condensation to accumulate and pool more easily.

Specific Heat Capacity: This is the amount of heat energy needed to increase the mass of a substance by one degree (or the amount of heat energy that must be lost to decrease it by one degree). For instance, wood has a specific heat capacity roughly four times more than steel for a pound of material. This indicates that a pound of steel will get much hotter than a pound of wood when exposed to a fixed amount of heat energy from the environment. In a metal building like a shipping container, this implies that the external temperature can have a drastic and rapid effect on the building's metal structure and skin. This means heating it quickly in the summer, but it can easily lose heat and drop below the dew point temperature under certain circumstances in the winter.

Thermal Conductivity: This measures the rate at which heat energy passes through a substance is measured by thermal conductivity. Steel has a thermal conductivity around 300 times greater than wood. This means that heat can pass fast through a shipping container's steel skin and structure, as well as through any thermal bridges that may exist. These thermal bridges could generate inefficient hot spots in the summer. In the winter, thermal bridges could create chilly patches within a container home, leading to condensation.

The two types of condensation you need to understand

Visible condensation: Moisture condenses on surfaces that can easily be seen just by walking around and without digging through walls, such as wall surfaces, windows, exposed pipes, and so on.

Concealed condensation: Sometimes called interstitial condensation, moisture that moves into and condenses inside the structure of a building in places like wall and ceiling cavities is known as interstitial condensation. Because it is hidden under wall coverings, this condensation is more harmful and hardest to deal with. Often, you don't even realize it's there until it's done a lot of damage. There are two major types of migrating moisture that cause concealed condensation:

Diffusion (Vapor Drive): This is a process by which water vapor migrates through a solid but porous material. For example, if one side of a gypsum board (drywall) is damp and the other is dry, moisture can penetrate the material despite the lack of obvious holes.

Infiltration (Air Leakage): This is a process by which air (including the water vapor it contains) migrates through visible holes in wall assemblies and materials and enters the wall assembly. Example problem areas include light fixtures, plumbing penetrations, electric switch plates, light fixtures, and the perimeter of windows and doors.

The essential thing to keep in mind is that if you have a visible condensation problem, you probably have concealed moisture inside your walls. If you find concealed condensation early and give your building time to 'dry out,' you may be fine. It is ongoing concealed condensation that never has time to evaporate that causes expensive and difficult issues.

The two (2) primary conditions in which condensation can occur in insulated shipping container homes

A cold environment with interior heating: The container's metal skin takes on the outer environment's chilly temperature. Moisture can be picked up by the heated interior air from the sources mentioned above. The moisture can infiltrate and diffuse its way through the wall system in some cases. It can form concealed condensation when it comes into contact with the cold outer metal skin. A vapor retarder could help in this case, but it can sometimes cause more difficulties than it solves!

A warm environment with interior air conditioning: The metal skin of the container absorbs the warm temperature of the exterior surroundings. When you open windows/doors or have an improperly sealed penetration, some warm, humid air enters the container and mixes with the interior air. If the container's interior is kept cold, some limited apparent condensation on interior surfaces is kept cool but exposed to warm, humid air. However, because the metal skin behind the interior wall surfaces is normally hot enough to be above the dewpoint temperature, there would be little chance of concealed condensation in this situation. In addition to cooling the newly introduced warm air, the air conditioner also reduces humidity by condensing the evaporator coil and exiting the structure. As a result, most of the moisture in the container would be removed automatically, and this situation is unlikely to occur very often.

What problems can condensation cause?

We've found that condensation results in a bit of water in the building's interior. But you may be asking yourself, "So what?" Well, that bit of water can cause more problems than you may think:

Metal deterioration: Rust can cause structural deterioration as well as being unappealing.

Masonry damage: Condensation and freeze-thaw cycles can cause cracking in rock, brick, and concrete.

Wood damage: moisture and Condensation in the presence of wood can cause wet rot (caused by specific strains of fungi), swelling, mold, and warping.

Coating and adhesive damage: Damage to varnishes, paints, and roofing/flooring adhesives are possible.

Equipment damage: Condensation can create chemical reactions that cause corrosion in materials such as fasteners, conditioning coils, and wiring. Moisture can also increase the conductivity of permeable insulators in electronic devices, causing short-circuiting and other problems.

Material staining: Water spots other obvious damage can stain building materials.

Insulation performance: Due to the high thermal conductivity of water, the presence of water in permeable or open-celled insulation reduces its R-value.

Slip hazards: Larger quantities of condensation that migrate or form onto floors can cause slipping hazards.

Health concerns: Condensation and moisture can cause unpleasant odors (usually from mold growth), allergy and asthma issues, a general lack of comfort and productivity, and may even contribute to Sick Building Syndrome.

Dealing with the moisture that causes condensation

You can regulate (1) the quantity of moisture entering the structure and (2) the amount of moisture leaving the structure:

Controlling moisture sources:

Showers: Use forced ventilation to ensure optimum ventilation.

Cooking: Use lids or an exhaust hood over your stove when cooking.

Drying clothes: Make sure the vent exhaust outside the building.

Building materials: During construction, avoid enclosure of wet building materials.

Exterior sealing: Melting snow, ice, rain, groundwater, surface runoff, and humid air should not be allowed to enter your building through roof and wall penetrations.

Plumbing leaks: Ensure there are not pinholes in pipes or leaking fittings and connections on any plumbing run where water can pool and evaporate.

<u>Removing interior moisture:</u>

Dehumidification: If you're in a cold area, use a portable electric dehumidifier to remove moisture from the air (the dehumidifiers will raise the air temperature).

Air conditioner "dry mode": If you're at a suitable temperature with too much relative humidity, use the dry mode setting that many windows and ductless AC units have to slow the fan and remove moisture from the air without cooling it considerably.

Ventilation: When the outside air's absolute humidity is lower, use windows, doors, and vents to replace inside air with outside air (and hence the air is drier).

A Note on Ventilation

Temperature control, condensation prevention, energy conservation, and indoor air quality are often in conflict, but ventilation impacts all of them. Bringing fresh air indoors, for example, can improve indoor air quality but may significantly alter humidity and temperature. Factors related to ventilation include:

Air quality: Due to the 'tightness' of container homes, ventilation is crucial even if moisture control is not required because it keeps the air from becoming stale (full of contaminants, odors, and containing lower oxygen levels).

Air conditioning confusion: Contrary to popular belief, most air conditioners do not provide outside air as part of their operation. Instead, they filter the indoor air, cool it, and remove moisture before recirculating it back into the structure. Ventilation must be provided by intentional (open windows, vent, and doors) and unintentional (building envelope leaks) means.

Ventilation rate: Ventilation can be represented by the cubic feet per minute (CFM) or the number of air changes per hour (ACH) of makeup air introduced into space. The recommendations vary by room/building use and are governed by various codes in various geographic areas, such as ASHRAE 62.1 & 62.2, IRC R303.4 & M1507, IMC 403.1 & 403.3, IECC R403.6 etc.

Relative humidity: Failure to provide sufficient ventilation might result in a cumulative increase in relative humidity over time in a sealed building. The absence of alternative strategies is outlined in the section above. Dry air from the outside is drawn into the building; the indoor air will be dehumidified. If humid air is drawn in, it can significantly increase the humidity load that the air conditioner must remove.

Air is continually traveling from high pressure to low-pressure areas, whether within or outside the building. Air and the water vapor in the air can be forced into or out of a positively or negatively pressurized (visible via a smoke test). Air will try to flow through wall penetrations when doors, windows, and vents are closed and may end up inside the wall envelope.

In condensation control, what role do vapor retarders and barriers play?

Vapor retarders are materials that reduce the rate of moisture diffusion and infiltration through a wall system. Vapor barriers are one type of vapor retarder. Vapor retarders are rated according to their measured permeance in 'perms.' The more perms there are, the more vapor can travel through the material. As a result, lower perms indicate a better block against vapor.

The Impact of Climate on Vapor Retarders

Originally, they were only used in cold climates, but they are now being utilized (often erroneously) in warmer climates. When used poorly, vapor retarders can aggravate moisture-related problems, which is the exact reverse of what they're supposed to do.

In a cold environment, vapor retarders are typically used on the inside (warm side) of a wall assembly (typically between the insulation and the drywall) to prevent the insulation and other wall materials from being exposed to the warmer, more humid inside air that could otherwise condense inside the wall. It works quite well in these cold climates.

Condensation from heated indoor air

Moisture from the heated indoor air condenses on drywall but cannot get through the vapor barrier to the outside.

Moisture would move through the wall system from the outside in, then encounter the cool vapor retarder (since it is close to the cold interior air) and condense inside the wall if used in this manner in a warm and humid environment.

Condensation from humid outdoor air

Condensation from the humid external air condenses on the vapor barrier and diffuses into the adjacent insulation and studs if they are porous.

As a result, in warm, humid areas, it's occasionally preferable to have the vapor retarder on the outer portion of the wall system or to have none at all. In fact, for places in the southern United States, Section 1404.3.1 of the 2018 IBC bans the use of a class I vapor retarder (and in some situations, even a class II) on the interior side of a wall system (Climate Zones 1-4, excluding Marine 4).

US Climate Zone Map

This may seem a little conflicting if you live in a place where it is hot and humid during some parts of the year and frigid at others. You're asking material to do different things at different periods of the year, which isn't very realistic.

Now that you've understood the vapor retarder conundrum in traditional construction, let's take a closer look at vapor retarders in shipping container homes.

Vapor Retarders in Shipping Container Homes

Remember that the most common container home condensation condition is a hot interior and a cold external environment, so we'll concentrate on that. Moisture from the sources indicated above can turn a warm interior into a warm and moist interior.

The recommendation above for vapor retarders in traditional buildings in a cold environment ignores the fact that with container construction, the container itself is a very effective vapor retarder in container construction. The vapor retarder formed by the container, on the other hand, is positioned on the exterior of the wall system, contrary to the recommendation!

Therefore, as often recommended, placing a vapor retarder on the warm side of an interior wall encapsulates the insulation between two vapor retarders. When moist air penetrates the wall system (which will, as a perfect vapor barrier, is nearly hard to achieve), it condenses on the container's cold metal walls, then diffuses into the insulation if it is permeable. Surrounded on both sides by vapor barriers, it will be difficult for the condensation to evaporate and insulation to dry. As previously mentioned, difficulties in the wall system are likely to arise.

Warm, moist air from the heated indoor environment condenses on the wall and finally migrates through it despite the vapor retarder, becoming stuck in the wall space.

If all of this sounds like a lot of bad news, fear not! Given the constraints imposed by shipping containers, there are numerous options for dealing with condensation.

Recommended approaches to shipping container condensation

Concealed condensation: When condensation does occur, make sure it's not concealed condensation. We don't want humid air, whether from outside or inside, entering the wall space, depending on where you live and the season. You want to maintain the cavity between the wall and the ceiling airtight. Any warm, humid air that penetrates the envelope goes into the interior area and only causes noticeable condensation.

Preventing diffusion into wall and ceiling cavities

Preventing infiltration into the ceiling and walls by being careful when installing plumbing, wiring, windows, doors, and other wall penetrations and properly sealing around wall penetrations.

Using insulation that is resistant to impregnation and moisture movement

Visible condensation: You can wipe away visible condensation with a towel if it continues, but if it reappears, you'll need to figure out why and how to fix it.

Dewpoint temperature: Condensation of any kind can only happen if the dewpoint temperature is below the surface temperature of the building envelope. The AC should immediately lower the RH, and any apparent condensation should evaporate. It's a little perplexing because temperature regulation also requires insulation.

Windows: Use premium insulated windows to help keep glass temperatures above the dewpoint temperature (in moist environments, warm, the condensation can appear on the outside of the window, strangely enough)

Thermal bridging: Keep anything (particularly metal) in the interior of your building from touching the container's exterior or metal frame to avoid thermal bridging. When possible, use thermal 'breaks' insulating materials placed between two pieces of metal to limit heat transfer. Ascertain that the thermal bridging item is surrounded by insulation, preventing it from coming into contact with the interior air.

Note on container condensation in cold and mixed-climate environments

Closed-cell insulation: We prefer Closed Cell Spray Polyurethane Foam (ccSPF) for almost all situations, especially colder climates. Once open cell foam or other porous insulation materials become wet, they are difficult to dry and become a breeding ground for mold and other bacteria. The closed-cell foam acts as an insulator and a vapor retarder, keeping moisture out of the wall cavity. The ccSPF, unlike a plastic sheet vapor retarder, is not readily broken, pierced, or cut, and it maintains its protection integrity. Additionally, the spray-in application forms a good seal by filling any gaps in corrugation, around outlets, and so on. We believe it is a worthwhile investment, even though it is a more expensive option.

Exterior insulation: Placing wall insulation outside the container is a less common choice because many individuals want their building to look like a shipping container. On the other hand, exterior insulation has several advantages, including increased interior space and less condensation inside the cavity. It is also not as important to use an expensive ccSPF since you don't have a lot of space, and porous insulation can dry out from the outside. If you decide to insulate the exterior, you'll need to cover the insulation with cladding to protect it from the elements and give it a more pleasing appearance. Vinyl or wood sliding, stucco, cement board, or even corrugated metal are all common choices.

Note on air conditioner short cycling

We previously explained how air conditioners could cool the air (remove sensible heat), remove moisture (remove latent heat), and lower humidity. However, the size of your air conditioner unit might have a significant impact on these processes.

Air conditioners remove moisture from the air by allowing the condenser, a cooling coil located inside the building, to cool below the dew point temperature. Water vapor condenses on the coil. A fan blows the air over the condenser and gently drips away down a condensate line, where it exits the building envelope. You've probably seen these outside soaking.

Whenever the air conditioner is turned on, it operates in a dry coil mode for several minutes until the condenser cools enough for water vapor to condense on it. However, if the coil is below the ambient temperature but above the dewpoint, air cooling can still occur before this temperature is reached.

A very small system will operate continuously and never reach the target temperature. That's bad. An oversized system will have short run durations throughout the day and spend more time in the dry coil phase before the condenser cools down sufficiently to remove water vapor from the air. This results in three issues. To begin with, there will be more humidity in your air than you like. Second, because starting as the most strenuous operation times are during s down are the most strenuous operation, your equipment will wear out faster. Third, you'll have spent extra upfront for the oversized system.

Do you want to know if your current air conditioner is the right size? Time how long your system runs on a hot afternoon with the thermostat set to your typical temperature. If it lasts fewer than 10 minutes (or comes on more than three times per hour) and the interior temperature is comfortable despite high interior relative humidity.

How can I check for possible condensation indications in my container?

To make any conclusive judgment regarding condensation, you must know the temperature, relative humidity, and dewpoint of the inside and outside air. Indoor temperature is a matter of personal discretion, but relative humidity should be kept between 30 and 60%.

You can get a reasonable indication of the outdoor conditions by finding a weather station close to you at Weather Underground. Still, the further away it is collected, the data is less accurate.

It's better first to determine the conditions at your location using a weather monitor to measure temperature and relative humidity, then calculate the dew point using a calculator or table.

A digital hygrometer/thermometer like this one can measure interior and exterior temperature and humidity with the base unit and a wireless measuring unit for the outdoors:

Another choice is a portable unit that can measure humidity and temperature anywhere that you carry it:

If you are concerned that some of the surfaces in your structure may be cooler and prone to condensation, an infrared laser thermometer might be particularly useful:

If you are concerned about CO2 levels in your building due to a perceived lack of ventilation, a desktop hygrometer/thermometer that includes CO2 monitoring is a good investment.

The origins of these common, unremarkable boxes are an intriguing tale. Who would have guessed that the materials we use to build houses today would have a huge impact on the world?

CHAPTER 9: GET OFF-GRID WITH A SHIPPING CONTAINER HOME

Off-the-grid living is becoming increasingly popular for various reasons, including social, political, and financial considerations. Having your self-sufficient piece of paradise that is not reliant on the water or electricity utility provides reliability and freedom.

What began as a simple campaign to disconnect from the power supply has evolved into something much larger. Living off the grid now often entails being self-sufficient and not relying on (or at least having a very limited reliance on). This implies no water, sewage, natural gas lines, cable connections, or electricity grid connections — in other words, no bills once it's built!

Off-grid living statistics vary; however, there could be up to a quarter of a million individuals living off-grid in the United States. Many people in third-world countries never can get onto the grid, implying that up to 1.7 billion people live off-grid globally.

A used shipping container can be a fantastic start to an off-grid
living project, whether by necessity or choice.

Why are shipping containers perfect for an off-grid living?

Shipping containers are great for constructing your off-grid living
space. They're inexpensive, practically universally available,
stackable, scalable, and simple to transport. Their solid construction
is built to resist the challenges of international shipping at sea, and
they may be cut and customized almost any way you want.

How to take your shipping container home off-the-grid

So far, we've discussed the advantages of off-grid shipping container homes, but what about the practical considerations?

<u>Electricity</u>

Living fully off the grid will require using some power generation, most commonly renewable energy sources found locally. These could be wind generation, photovoltaic solar power, tidal or wave generation, geothermal or hydroelectric power, with solar power being the easiest to set up with solar power being the easiest to implement. Other options, such as utilizing a commercially available diesel generator, are less environmentally beneficial, but expenses can quickly add up if you use a lot of fuel.

The main issue is that you have to use the energy as soon as it is produced, and there are few options for balancing the load or storing it because high-capacity batteries are enormous, heavy, and expensive. Change, however, appears to be on the horizon, with Tesla Motors releasing a brand new product, the Tesla Powerwall, that would likely make off-grid life a lot more accessible to the average person. This device takes energy generated by solar panels during the day (when most people are out of the house and not using power – except for air conditioning and refrigerators) and allows it to be used during peak demand – between 5 and 10 p.m. and in the mornings when people take their daily showers – effectively balancing the load.

While these and devices are not currently commercially accessible worldwide, it is only a matter of time before they are, and you will likely see a far bigger number of homeowners around the world living off the grid, at least for electricity. This type of product allows you to build a shipping container home with a full electrical setup while remaining completely off the grid. Using energy-efficient appliances and LED lighting will also help you save money on electricity daily.

<u>Water Supply & Sewerage</u>

So, once you've figured out how to get and dispose of your water and liquid waste products safely and legally, you'll need to figure out how to get and dispose of them once you've figured out your sustainable, off-grid power supply. This will all depend on where your off-grid container house is located and whether or not you are near a spring or a source of groundwater (where you can drill a well). If you live in an area with a decent amount of rain, rainwater could be a viable option. You'll want to live far away from big sources of pollution, such as factories and highways. Rainwater can be collected by gutters from a roof and stored in a large tank or cistern. After collecting, all water must be filtered to human drinking water standards to guarantee that it is safe to consume, though this may not be necessary if the water is only used for washing.

It's a little more difficult to get rid of wastewater and other sewage. There are a few options for this, but composting toilets or a septic tank system are the most frequent. Septic tanks are subject to local government restrictions, and while they are legal in certain regions, they are prohibited or extensively regulated in others. Septic tanks collect wastewater and allow microorganisms to break down waste before releasing it, whereas composting toilets employ a unique design combined with wood chips to convert waste into compost. Some people use this on their gardens, but others warn against the dangers of doing so — it should never be used on any food-producing gardens. Both must be professionally installed and maintained, with specific attention paid to ensuring that any items used are environmentally safe and appropriate for septic or composting systems.

Heating & Cooking

If you live in an area with extreme temperature fluctuations, you'll almost certainly need to consider heating. The first and most crucial thing you can do is properly insulate your container home to avoid severe temperature variations. Electrically fired heating is definitely out of the question because you'll be generating your power. Unless you have a ready supply of sustainable timber nearby, installing a fireplace can be a nice idea, even if it is a little ecologically unfriendly.

A gas stove is perfect for cooking. Simply set up a system in which a gas bottle, similar to the one used in a BBQ, is stored outside of your kitchen area under a covered area, and a hose is connected to your gas stove. Keep a spare cylinder filled at all times, and refill whenever you return to town for fuel.

When it comes to cooking time, using a gas stove instead of an electrical one will lessen the load on your power system, or if you want to use a standard element, try purchasing one that is split between gas and electrical power. That way, even if you can keep cooking even if you are low on power.

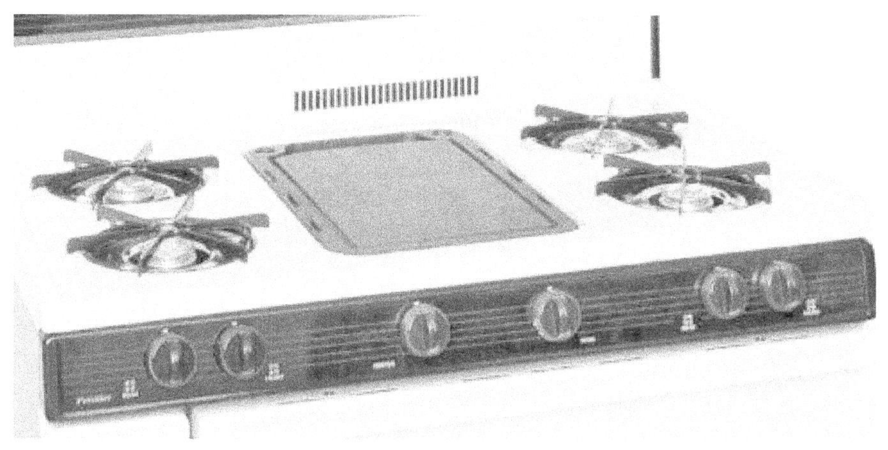

Rubbish and Food Scraps

You may not have access to a waste collection service, depending on how far off the grid you are. In this instance, you'll want to start by reducing your consumption of packaged goods, then recycle what you can and compost what you can't. Remember that devices like an Insinkerator may not be viable if you use a septic tank or composting system to dispose of your waste. Waste that cannot be recycled or composted will have to be burned in an incinerator.

Off-Grid Food

The idea of having your food supply off-grid is often overlooked. Planting a garden that provides you with most of your food requirements can make your home even more self-sufficient and eliminate the need to go to the shop every week for staple foods. Consider a "Green Roof" to save space while still allowing you to grow the essentials for a healthy lifestyle while also providing more green spaces and making your home more environmentally friendly.

What about the total costs?

This can be surprising, and people may experience "sticker shock." Yes, container homes are less costly than conventional buildings, but some drawbacks are associated with living off the grid. Keep in mind that these costs will be recouped over time when you stop paying your utility bills, as well as the value you obtain from being completely self-sufficient.

The costs of sewerage, off-grid power, and other systems add up, but they are getting more and more cost-effective every day with technological advancements. Expect it to be more expensive, but it will save you money in the long run.

CHAPTER 10: SHIPPING CONTAINER FLOORING

"Should I remove the floor in my shipping container?" is one of the most often asked questions about shipping container flooring.

One of the simplest methods to save money when turning shipping containers into homes or offices is to preserve the container's original flooring. The main issue with using the existing floor, however, is safety.

Tropical hardwoods which have been treated with crude pesticides are commonly used as flooring in shipping containers. These harsh chemicals are harmful to people; the existing plywood flooring should not be used.

Shipping Container Flooring

Consider the original purpose of shipping containers to comprehend shipping container flooring. They were created to endure the rigors of long-distance ocean travel while also protecting the contents of the containers.

The most common flooring used in shipping containers is one-inch marine plywood manufactured from tropical hardwoods like Keruing or Apitong. These hardwoods, unfortunately, attract a wide range of pests.

The wooden flooring is coated with pesticides to prevent insects and other critters from causing damage to the goods.

This is a valid system for transporting goods, but it is dangerous when used to construct a home or office. These severe insecticides are toxic to humans, particularly children and the elderly, and should not be used in shipping container homes.

The good news is that many of the most dangerous pesticides, like Aldrin and Dieldrin, have been banned or severely restricted. However, other pesticides are still used on virtually all container flooring.

According to the Container Owners Association, tropical hardwood is still used in a substantial percentage of shipping container floors.

While many shipping container manufacturers consider alternate flooring options like steel and bamboo, your shipping container flooring is likely to have been treated with pesticides.

How to Check Your Shipping Container Floors

If you're lucky enough to buy your containers brand new, you'll be able to make some special demands. You have the option of not having the plywood floors treated with pesticides. You can also request that a different form of floorings, such as steel or bamboo, be used instead of plywood.

However, most people build utilizing used shipping containers rather than buying new ones. If this is the case, what should be done?

When constructing a building out of used shipping containers with treated plywood flooring, some detective work will be required to determine whether the floors are safe to keep.

Locate the consolidated data plate, also known as the container safe convention plate, to confirm which chemicals were utilized to treat your floor. This plate is usually attached to the front door of the container.

A section labeled "timber component treatment" can be seen on the plate. This section is divided into three parts:

• Part 1: IM (immunity)

- Part 2: Treatment chemical

- Part 3: Treatment date

Once you have discovered the information regarding the chemicals used on your container, determine whether the floors will need to be removed and replaced. Review the World Health Organization's pesticide categorization to learn more about the toxicity of the chemicals used.

It's important to remember that the data plate won't tell you everything. For example, if the container's floor was damaged and replaced at some point, the plate will not reflect this. Furthermore, the data plate will not reveal what was shipped inside the container or whether any harsh chemicals were spilled inside the container during its journey across the oceans.

Should You Remove The Plywood Floor?

Most people remove the original plywood flooring and replace it with new flooring. But, in the end, it's up to you and your budget to make the decision.

Removing the original flooring and replacing it with new flooring is the safest option. This will provide you with peace of mind and the assurance that you are making the right decision for your family and friends.

How to Remove the Plywood Floor

The floor bolts must first be cut out with a hand saw or reciprocating saw before the plywood can be removed. The bolts are generally spaced every twelve inches and are fixed along with the cross members.

Once all of the floor bolts have been removed, lift the floor panels up and out of the container with a pry bar. This is a relatively simple task, but it can take a long time! Once the plywood has been removed, you can now lay your new flooring.

Another benefit of removing the original flooring is that you may insulate underneath the container once the floor has been removed. You can simply reach the floor's cross members and apply spray foam or panel insulation now that the flooring has been removed!

It can be difficult to insulate underneath the container without removing the flooring. You'll need to use a crane and then spray foam to lift your containers in most cases.

How to Treat the Original Plywood Floor

This section is for you if you've decided to retain and treat your original plywood floor.

The biggest worry with keeping the original plywood flooring is the toxic fumes released by the insecticides used to eradicate the pests. There is still a risk, even though the chemical potency will fade after a few years.

The most common solution is to apply epoxy to the flooring. This will act as a sealant, preventing pesticide vapors from escaping.

When selecting an epoxy, be sure it's solvent-free and, most essential, that it's safe to use on wood.

Clean the plywood with isopropyl alcohol before applying the epoxy.

As a precaution, make sure there is enough ventilation when applying the isopropyl alcohol and epoxy. These vapors are poisonous and can be very strong.

If you don't want to use epoxy, a non-breathable flooring underlayment is an alternative. Larry from Sea Container Cabin decided to use a non-breathable flooring layer when converting his used shipping containers years ago.

The flooring underlayment was simply laid down Over the original plywood container floors. The underlayment was then covered with tiles.

Concrete is another alternative that we've seen used. Concrete, like the underlayment mentioned earlier, is used to 'seal' the plywood flooring. Before the concrete is laid, polyethylene plastic is placed on top of the original plywood. After that, the concrete is poured on top of the plastic.

Most shipping containers have tropical hardwood plywood floors. Before being loaded into shipping containers, this hardwood is treated with possibly dangerous pesticides.

This makes the containers great for transportation, but it also means that they aren't suitable for living in because the pesticides used to treat the wooden floors might harm humans.

It is a personal decision whether or not to keep the original flooring in your container. It all relies on the history of your shipping container, your budget, and your taste.

ROOF FOR YOUR SHIPPING CONTAINER HOME

The decision to implement a roof to your container is based on both personal style preferences and budgetary considerations. Not roofing your container will save you money at first. However, installing a roof and insulating can save you money on energy bills in the long run.

Because hot air rises, most of the heat lost in your home will escape through your roof.

Consider that having a roof helps you insulate the inside of the roof, allowing you to maintain and keep the inside temperature stable. A roof with an overhang prevents rain from falling on your windows and eliminates the need for a drip bar above them.

Different Roof Styles

Shed

A shed roof, like the one pictured below, is essentially a sloped roof. The benefits of using a shed-style roof include its low cost and ease of construction. This type of roof may be built and erected in a matter of days. Solar panels are a good fit for the long, sloping roof.

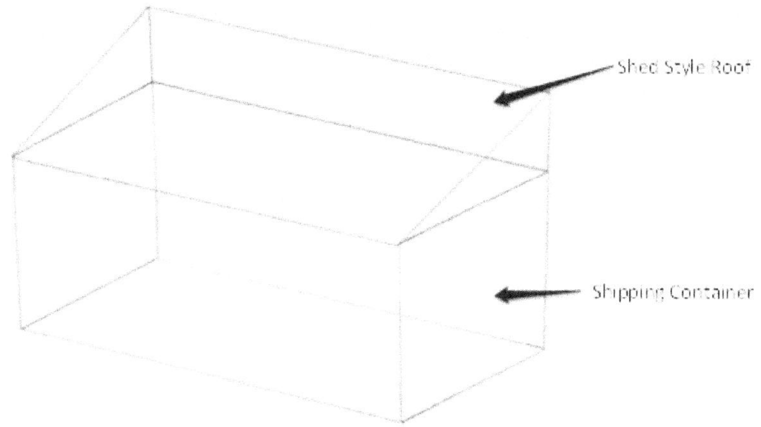

Weld right-angled steel plates across the length of the shipping container on both sides to install a shed-style roof for your shipping container. Attach a wooden beam to the steel plates on each side of the container roof. The trusses should be screwed into this beam. The basic structure of the roof is starting to take shape now. To finish the roof's structure, attach steel bars or purlins for structural support across the trusses. Simply add 20 foot long purlins to the trusses for this phase, and you're done. Your trusses will then require bracing to protect you from the wind.

For specifics, you'll have to rely on your structural engineer. This expert engineer will be able to provide you with advice on the precise load-bearing requirements for your roof. Natural strains exerted on your roofs, such as rain, wind, and snow loads, are factored into this figure, which varies by region.

You can use galvanized metal sheets, shingles, or coated steel sheets to cover your roof. Coated steel is the most durable, but galvanized metal sheets are easy to install and long-lasting.

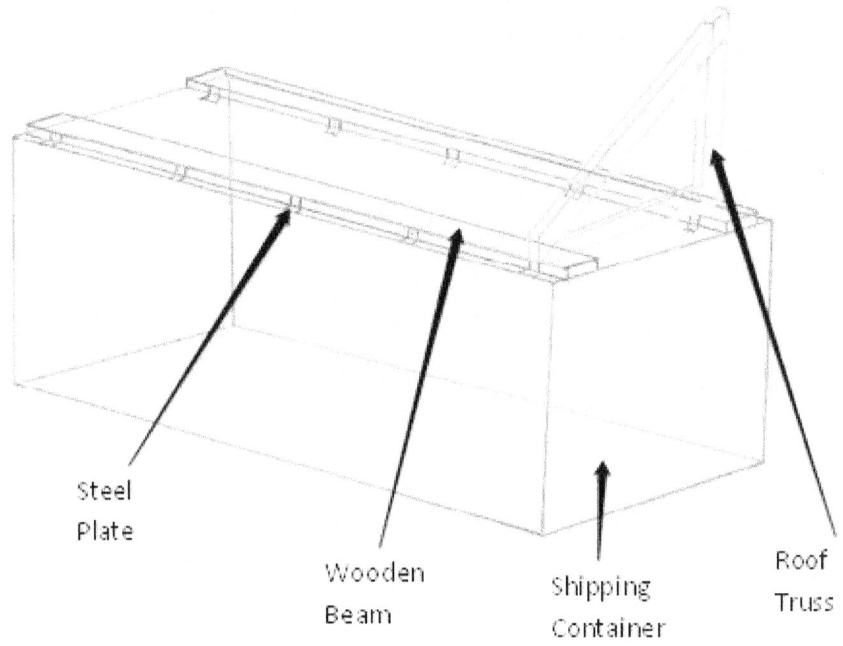

The next step is to make sure your roof has enough ventilation. To achieve this, your trusses should overhang the container, as shown below. Install a fascia and soffit board underneath your trusses. Air should be able to flow in and out of the roof through the soffit board, which should have at least an inch air gap in the middle, covered with wire mesh.

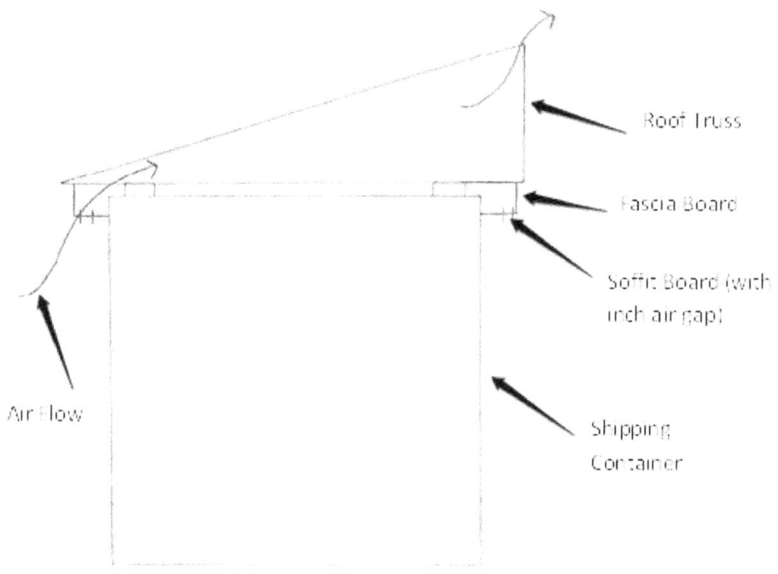

Make sure the gable ends have enough airflow. To achieve this, simply cut slots in the steel with a disc cutter. This will allow air to flow freely through the roof, preventing heat traps and condensation, both of which can lead to corrosion.

Gable

The next option is to use a gable roof, as shown below. When most people think of a traditional home, they see a gable-styled roof. It has a distinct triangle appearance. The benefit of a gable roof is that it has a slanted roof that allows for excellent water drainage. This reduces the likelihood of leaks and extends the life of your roof. Its popularity stems from the fact that it offers greater ceiling space than other roof layouts.

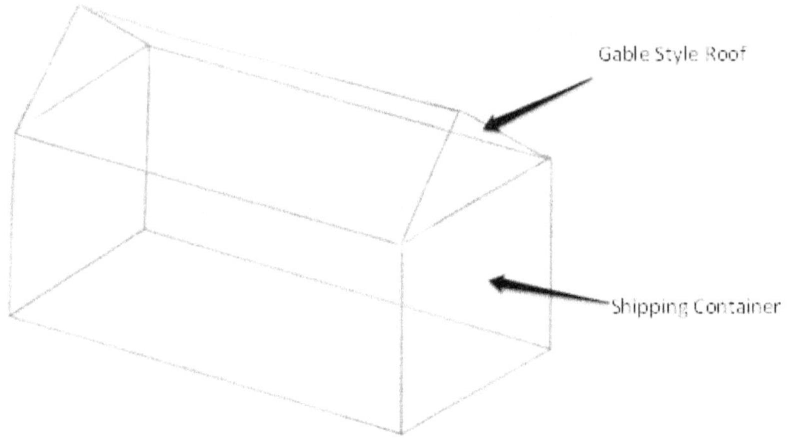

The stages for installing a shed-style roof are identical to the stages for installing this roof.

To install a gable-style roof on your shipping container, weld right-angled steel plates across the length of the shipping container on both sides. Attach a wooden beam to the steel plates on each side of the container roof. The roof's basic structure is starting to shape as you screw your trusses into these wooden beams. Install purlins across the trusses to finish the roof's structure.

You can use galvanized metal sheets, shingles, or coated steel sheets, just like the shed-style roof.

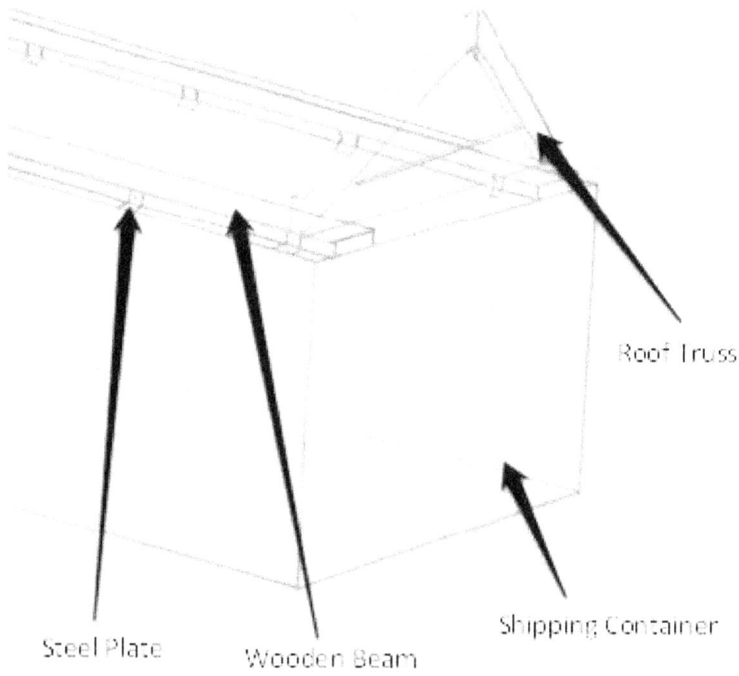

Now check to see if the roof has enough ventilation. The trusses should overhang the container, as shown below. After that, you can install fascia and soffit boards beneath your trusses. Air should be able to flow in and out of the roof through the soffit board, which should have at least an inch air gap in the middle, covered with wire mesh.

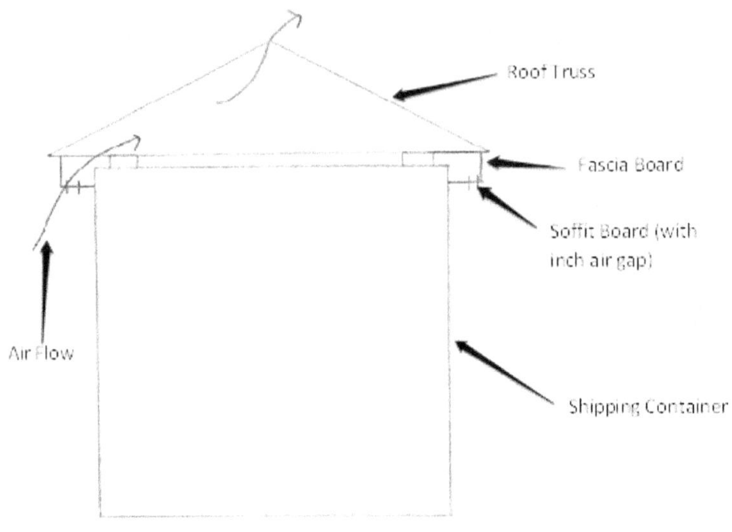

Flat

Some people may be happy with a flat roof, which the shipping container already has. Although it is cheaper not to roof your shipping container, you risk water pooling on the roof.

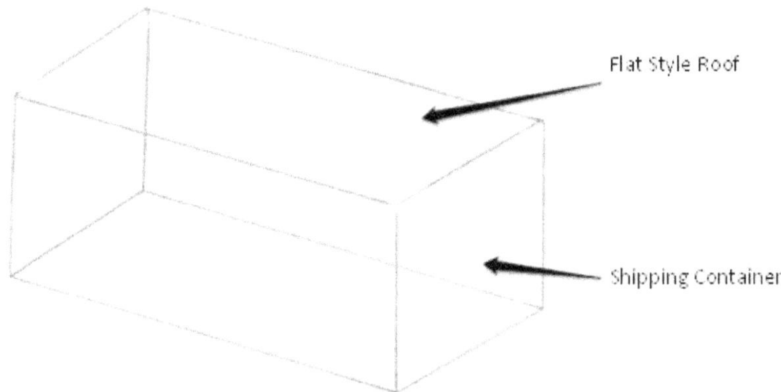

If you don't want to roof your containers, you should put up a rapid safety barrier. Place a tarpaulin sheet on the container's roof and cover it with asphalt rolls. This will act as an additional barrier between the dampness and the container's roof.

The Benefits of Having a Structural Engineer

Regardless of the roof type you pick, work with your structural engineer to calculate the load-bearing needs of your roof.

They will achieve this by calculating the roof's dead, living, and transitory loads.

- The dead load refers to the total weight of all the materials used to construct the roof (i.e., purlins, trusses, roof tiles).
- The live load refers to the weight of any equipment and persons involved in the roof installation.
- The transient load refers to all-natural forces exerted on the roof, such as wind, rain, and snow.

Your roof's load-bearing capacity is the maximum weight that the roof's structure can carry without collapsing.

Each area will encounter different challenges. For instance, areas prone to high winds will need roofs with additional truss bracing. Warmer areas with a light breeze don't need a roof with solid structural capability, but they need insulation benefits.

To prevent condensation, all roof types need appropriate ventilation.

CONCLUSION

Building using shipping containers is still a relatively new architecture and construction method, but the trend is still strong.

The development of a container home for shipping can be one of your most satisfying experiences. Cost-saving and mobility are some of the main benefits of building your home using shipping containers. They can also be constructed at incredible speed. They are cheap, easy to install, and environmentally friendly; we save about 3500KG of steel for every shipping container cycled up.

However, the prospective thinkers celebrate. Homeowners have also used containers to build a house without ending up with thousands of dollars of debt. The shop owners and some mobile utilities, and low-income housing developers have also joined the party.

Shipping containers have a place in the world of construction and architecture, but their inherent flaws and restrictions cannot be overlooked. With more experience and time, construction problems will be more effectively addressed, and the trend in cargo technology will continue to grow.

Just as in traditional housing, it is important you have the right amount of knowledge and information before you build a container.